Michael Brown, Jr.

didn't have to die

by

Ken Dye

the Peppertree Press

Sarasota, Florida

Other titles by Ken Dye:
Shadow of the Arch
Beyond the Shadow of the Arch

Copyright © Ken Dye, 2015

All rights reserved. Published by the Peppertree Press, LLC.
The Peppertree Press and associated logos are trademarks of
the Peppertree Press, LLC.

No part of this publication may be reproduced, stored in a retrieval system,
transmitted in any form or by any means, electronic, mechanical, photocopying,
recording, or otherwise, without prior written permission of the publisher and
author/illustrator. Graphic design by Rebecca Barbier.

For information regarding permission,
call 941-922-2662 or contact us at our website:
www.peppertreepublishing.com or write to:
the Peppertree Press, LLC.
Attention: Publisher
1269 First Street, Suite 7
Sarasota, Florida 34236

ISBN: 978-1-61493-382-3

Library of Congress Number: 2015916094

Printed November 2015

DEDICATION

To the men and women of the law enforcement agencies, throughout the St. Louis area, that stood shoulder to shoulder in the face of bullets, bottles and bad guys. Your professionalism, dedication and resolute determination to successfully conclude the Ferguson unrest reflects great credit upon the profession of Law Enforcement.

Blessed are the peacemakers.

TABLE OF CONTENTS

THE INCIDENT

In Ferguson, Missouri, a St. Louis suburb, it's Saturday, August 9, 2014. Michael Brown and his friend, Dorian Johnson, just finished smoking a quantity of marijuana-laced cigars. The two wanted Cigarillos to handcraft these cigars. Being righteous businessmen, they know the finished product retails for somewhere in the vicinity of twenty-five dollars around Canfield Green Apartments, where they both lived. As with any densely populated housing site, some residents are law-abiding, working individuals, and families—others, just the opposite.

11:43— Brown, who tips the scale at about 300 pounds and stands six feet-four inches, and Johnson, a smaller soul, enter the Ferguson Market.

Both approach the counter, where Brown grabs a box containing Swisher Sweet cigars. Both head for the front door.

The clerk, a middle-aged man, attempts to stop the two and retrieve the merchandise. Brown assaults the clerk by pushing and shoving him into a potato chip rack. The store's video surveillance system captures this encounter. Brown's actions constitute the elements for the offense of Robbery, 2nd degree.

11:53— Ferguson police dispatcher receives call for "stealing in progress" at Ferguson Market. Nineteen seconds later, dispatcher broadcasts a description of one of the suspects: black male, white T-shirt, running towards the Quick Trip.

Four minutes later, additional information regarding the other suspect is broadcast: black male, red Cardinal baseball cap, white T-shirt, yellow socks, and khaki shorts.

12:00— Officer Darren Wilson goes back in service after attending to a sick child call.

While on that particular call, he hears the broadcast of the subjects wanted for the stealing in progress, the radio transmission, intermittent and broken, possibly due to the construction of the building he's in. Additionally, Officer Wilson is working on his assigned call of a sick infant. After leaving that call, as he is en route to meet his girlfriend for lunch, he observes two people walking in the middle of the road. He slows down and says, "Why don't you guys walk on the sidewalk?"

Michael Brown, Jr. replies, "Fuck what you have to say!"

12:02— Wilson radios, "Frank 21, put me out on Canfield with two and send me another car." His call prompted two other cars to proceed to his location. Wilson attempts to stop Brown and Johnson.

As Wilson tries to open the door, Brown slams it shut.

Brown charges the open window of the police SUV, striking Officer Wilson with a closed fist and gains access to the interior. Brown then attempts to grab Officer Wilson's gun. Brown manages to extract the weapon from the holster and points it towards Wilson's right leg. During the struggle, Wilson's radio switches from the regular police channel to a listen-only mode, as Wilson fights to retain control of his weapon.

Wilson is able to regain control of his weapon and fires one shot, striking Brown in the left hand and forearm. Brown exits or is pushed from the SUV. Before Wilson exits the SUV to pursue the suspect, he broadcasts: "Shots fired, send all cars." Since his radio was switched inadvertently to the listen-only setting, this call was not received.

Several feet from the SUV, Brown turns and faces Wilson, makes a grunting sound, lowers his arms to a stance similar to that of a linebacker, and begins running toward the officer.

Wilson fires several times, striking Brown in center mass and top of his head. Brown dies at the scene. By this time, other units arrive.

12:07— A woman wails in the background as an officer calls, "Get us more units over here, there's going to be a problem."

Ferguson police department chief, Tom Jackson arrives, quickly assesses the scene, and calls the St. Louis county police for additional assistance.

The police dispatcher broadcasts, "All tactical operations units proceed to Ferguson, switch to Riot Channel A."

Michael Brown, Jr. did not have to die that hot, muggy August day in Ferguson, Missouri.

GROWING THREAT

The mob mentality took root almost immediately after the shooting of Michael Brown.

Testimony, ballistic, autopsy reports, and physical evidence will disprove many of the statements made by a number of Ferguson and North St. Louis residents that did not know Mike Brown, Adrian Johnson, or any family members, close or extended.

People who live in or near the scene of the incident did, in fact, make up stories about Michael Brown being executed by Officer Wilson and pressured others to go along with the story, to lie and mislead the police investigation. Failure to comply with the bogus story or not keeping quiet could be harmful to individuals and their families.

A number of members of the growing crowd display weapons in their waistbands. They threaten casual observers to go along with the false representations being transmitted on social media and local and national news outlets.

By the time homicide detectives arrive on the scene, a large crowd of bystanders and a considerable uniformed police presence is in place. The crowd includes both Brown's mother and stepfather. Many of the individuals are upset and express their frustration by yelling obscenities and threats, and attempt to encroach on the crime scene.

The scene grows worse as the investigation continues. Several sizable groups of hostile individuals gather around the perimeter and interrupt the process a number of times, directing death threats at police officers.

Several people in the crowd fire gunshots, putting those on the frontline in a precarious position.

Numerous witnesses describe intimidation from the local population, as well as falsification of testimony. One witness tells police she did not want to become involved for fear of retaliation. She says, "I know these people, I have to live here."

Another female witness states to police, "I don't know nuthin'."

An adult male near the scene comments to St. Louis county detectives as they walk by that he witnessed the incident and the officer "was in the right and did what he had to do." He adds, "... the statement being made by others in the complex are inaccurate." The detectives momentarily stop to speak to this person, who was clearly uncomfortable speaking with detectives. He indicates he will not make any further comments and refuses to identify himself. As a practical matter and in reality, who on earth could blame him?

Two other witnesses, one male and one female, say they are afraid to speak about what they saw. Both indicate they were worried about retaliation from the people who live in the area—a valid concern.

One bystander begins crying and says she will not talk about it. The man next to her says that he "saw Brown inside the officer's vehicle, but he walked away. When he turns back around, Brown is moving quickly towards the officer." The witness reports hearing several more gunshots. Once again, it is interesting to note that both witnesses refuse to provide taped statements.

Another witness tells police, "she has been talking to her neighbors about the incident, and her neighbors are upset at what they believe happened." She relates to detectives that her neighbors' beliefs are inconsistent with what she witnessed.

Yet another witness advises police, "I was present when the whole thing went down and I saw exactly what happened. That officer was correct in doing what he did." The subject further states, "The information being broadcast by the news outlets is nothing but a big-ass lie. The information is not at all accurate and there are blatant lies being told by the people being interviewed. The events they describe are way different from what I saw and I was right there. There were plenty of people present when that boy got shot, but they are telling lies when the media interviews them— totally false comments."

Yet another witness to the incident tells police he has already told detectives from the St. Louis county police and the FBI that he is not willing to discuss the matter formally, but is willing to discuss his fears. He says,

"Threats were made to the residents in the Canfield Green Apartment Complex. Notes had been posted on the various apartment buildings threatening people not to talk to the police and gunshots are still being fired every night."

This person tells investigators at least ten people observed the entire incident. He refuses to share the names with police.

This witness also states that while they were both in the street, "The officer told Brown, no less than ten times, to get down on the ground. Brown never had his hands raised."

In FBI interviews, witnesses repeat the accusations as to what they believed happened—not what actually happened.

This individual, who would eventually become a grand jury witness, initially said, "Brown was shot from behind. I seen the officer stand over him and empty his clip in his head."

This message resonated well with the newsies. Anything for ratings.

One witness advises investigators: "If folks can latch onto something, then they embellish it, 'cause they want something to do. This is something. It's like giving the OK now, we got something we can get into ... the majority of them do not work. They all the time sit around and get high all day. Two people have never seen these folks before. In the whole time I was out there, I never saw them, and I sit out there a lot. They came up threatening, 'Hey, y'all better not say nothin', y'all snitching and all.' "

A future grand jury witness adds that within one minute of the shooting, " ... there were 70 to 80 people saying things that didn't happen, and they start embellishing their statements when the stepfather shows up. They lie when they say the officer ran up behind him and shot him in the back. They lie when they say he had his hands straight up in the air. They lie when they say that Brown was shot when down. They have the mindset of what happened. They are set that they are looking for a reason to explode, that's what they want, 'cause they don't have nothing to do ... they have nothing else to do. They are running all day, drinking, and getting high all day—we see this all the time."

Testimony shows that some witnesses routinely exaggerate their accounts and change them to fit the autopsy report as that report breaks in the media.

Many witnesses lie about seeing the events at all—a mighty load of information and statements for the detectives and FBI agents to untangle and seek out the truth. This requires several re-interviews with all who gave voluntary statements, somewhere in the vicinity of two-hundred. Although arduous and time-consuming, information must be reviewed, re-reviewed and double-checked to ensure it corresponds with the physical and forensic evidence, which is a daunting task, but one they undertake with professionalism and integrity.

Grand jury testimony and the United States department of justice memorandum on the Brown shooting verify the truth. Michael Brown attacked Officer Wilson. Wilson did not grab Brown by the neck or shirt while he sat in his police SUV.

How would one determine this you ask? Good question ... Wilson's DNA, not found on Brown's shirt. Dorian Johnson, Brown's friend, states during the early portion of the investigation that Brown and the officer were involved in a "tug-of-war" with Brown's shirt. If this had happened, Officer Wilson's DNA would have been on the shirt. Wilson's DNA is not found on Brown's T-shirt. However, Brown's DNA is found on Wilson's uniform pants, his weapon, and the interior of the police unit.

The fact that Michael Brown was not shot in the back is verified by three separate autopsies.

Does any of this matter to the growing mob? Not at this time. The social media is abuzz with "first-hand" accounts—a cause célèbre for activists and thugs everywhere.

At an impromptu interview early in the operation Chief Jon Belmar of the St. Louis county police department is asked, "Have you ever seen anything like this?" The chief replies, "I haven't even heard of anything like this."

SPINNING

St. Louis county police units roll into the crucible and begin stringing crime scene tape across the street and sidewalk, the center of attention being the body of Michael Brown, Jr. lying on the street. His red St. Louis Cardinal hat is upside down, in plain view of the growing number of spectators. A blue and gold fabric bracelet also lays on the street.

Privacy sheets soon block the view of the body of Michael Brown, Jr.

The commentary emanating from the mob becomes more violent. "The muthfucking police shot that boy." "Kill the police!""His hands was up, man—they didn't have to shoot that boy."

In this era of instant communication, Facebook, Twitter, and texting among what seems like everyone propel information carrying false narratives of the incident, as grand jury testimony will later prove.

The crowd grows. Periodic gunshots resonate throughout the area.

The county police crime scene detectives work the area—photographs, measurements, the blood trail—everything is recorded and photographed. The yellow evidence indicators dot the roadway and crime scene. This painstaking, intensive investigation becomes crucial as the matter progresses. About an hour into the initial investigation, a series of gunshots originating from the interior of the gathering crowd erupt. All activity ceases until the officer in charge of the CSI feels it is safe to continue, about an hour's delay.

The body must remain in its original state to take measurements and collect evidence in relation to the body. The crime scene investigators have only one shot at getting this right. Everyone at the scene knows this is the real McCoy and an extremely big case. No O. J. Simpson crime scene mistakes on this one. Everything exact, precise.

The St. Louis county police crime scene unit and the activities they conducted the day of the incident have not been challenged or compromised by anyone. They must have got the thing right. A professional and thorough police organization indeed.

The TAC sergeant deploys the cops along the yellow and black tape. It's soon clear this is trouble. Big trouble.

Ferguson police chief Tom Jackson activates a mutual aid agreement with neighboring police departments—Code 1000, the code for a riot or potential riot. Police officers flood the area with law enforcement in the hopes of containing the disturbance. The area is soon crawling with cops from a number of jurisdictions.

To the untrained eye, it looks like a mess. The officers deploy in a circle to protect the evidence and those feverously working the site conceal Michael Brown by placing privacy sheets around his body.

Police officer Darren Wilson drives to the Ferguson police department. He speaks briefly with St. Louis county crimes against persons detectives before being taken to an area hospital for treatment of facial swelling and lacerations to his face and neck.

The news trucks arrive. All local stations soon broadcast images of an increasingly angry and ugly crowd. On camera, the newsies, scrunching up their most thoughtful and serious faces, begin to talk ... and talk ... and speculate ... and talk.

Unarmed black teenager, shot and killed by a white police officer—a term we will all hear over and over. Can't get enough of that.

What the newsies fail to tell the spellbound public is that the officer shot the unarmed black teenager AFTER he attempted to get the officer's gun. A fact the grand jury and the justice department will find out.

Against the backdrop of chaotic activity, a resident of the Canfield Greens apartment complex, who will subsequently become a grand jury witness, is walking near the location of the incident. He is able to see the events unfold as it happened.

He views the struggle in Wilson's police car, with Brown confronting Wilson inside the car. He sees Dorian Johnson. Sees him run away when the officer becomes the subject of the attack by Michael Brown, Jr.

On Monday, August 11th, two days after the shooting he goes to the Ferguson police department where he is interviewed by two St. Louis county crimes against persons detectives. He states, "After seeing the rioting, I called the St. Louis county police. I just felt bad about the situation. I knew that I needed to come forward to let the truth be told. I felt uncomfortable then just walking past all the protesting that was going on, but I knew it was the right thing to do. It is an unfortunate situation, but I know God put me in this situation for a reason."

He relays to the detectives that "immediately after the shooting, I observe the chaotic situation and how it got worse so quickly—the different points of view—it didn't add up to what I actually witnessed. I feel very uncomfortable and … I would probably estimate I was down on the scene maybe five to ten minutes … just observing everything and how the uproar came about so quickly. When I started to say what I saw, some folks in the crowd became verbally abusive, with three thug-type guys coming up to me and showing me their guns stuck in their waistbands. As I go home, I see more and more people pouring into Ferguson. Most of them I never saw before. They were coming by the carloads. When it got dark, all the rioting started. The crowd was throwing stuff at the police, who held their ground.

" … I just sees Mr. Brown inside the police officer's window. It appears as though some sort of confrontation is taking place … that seems to take seconds … I'm not sure how long. The first shot was let loose and after that, Mike Brown comes out of the window and takes off running. So my initial thought is that—wow, did I just witness this young guy kill a police officer?"

"Half Mike Brown's body, his feet still planted on the ground, his upper body inside the window in a leaning motion inside the window, his upper body was inside. It just looks out of the norm with somebody leaning over inside the police officer's car."

The witness further explains after the firing of that shot, Michael Brown and his friend Adrian Johnson take off down Canfield Drive. Officer Wilson remains in the car briefly, then pursues with his gun drawn, but not firing at Brown.

"Brown then turns and runs full charge toward Wilson. He stops, turns, and does some sort of body gesture. I'm not sure what it is, but I know it's a body gesture. And I can say for sure, he never puts his hands up. After the gesture, he runs towards the officer, full charge. The officer fires several shots at him and to give an estimate, I would say he fires roughly around five or six shots at Mike Brown, who is still coming towards the officer and at this point, I'm thinking—wow, is this officer missing Mike Brown at such close range? Brown continuously comes forward in a charging motion, but at one point, he starts to slow down and then comes to a stop. When Brown stops, that's when the officer ceases fire. Then Mike Brown starts to charge once more at him. When he charges, the officer returns fire with, I would say, an estimate of three to four shots. And that's when Mike Brown finally collapses."

This future grand jury witness speaks from the heart, trying to bring some comfort to Michael Brown's family: "I come forward to bring closure to the family and also for the police officer, 'cause … with me knowing actually what happened … I know it is gonna be a hard case and a hard thing to prove with so many people saying the opposite of what I actually seen. I just want to bring closure to the family, not thinking that—hey … they got away with murdering my son. I do know that there is corruption in some police departments, but I believe that this is not the case here. And I just want to bring closure to the family."

It is interesting to note that this interview is conducted prior to the completion of an autopsy, the grand jury report, or the department of justice memorandum absolving Ferguson police officer Darren Wilson of violating any federal statute.

In his recorded statement, the recollection of events parallels the testimony of Darren Wilson's grand jury appearance on September 16, 2014. For example, he describes Wilson pursuing, but not firing at Brown until Brown turns around and charges. He also describes the initial series of shots, where Brown stops, next Wilson stops firing, and then Brown resumes his charge. Wilson gave essentially, the same testimony, talking about a pause between a first and second round of shots, only to be forced to fire by Brown's final rush. Had he succeeded in obtaining the officer's weapon, Big Mike would have had the opportunity to injure or kill the officer. Big Mike already had one attempt to get Wilson's weapon … he didn't deserve a second chance.

The witness had a clear view of the events. He gives testimony that not only coincides with that of Officer Wilson, but also the ballistic evidence. He did not know Big Mike or Officer Wilson. For those that think it's important, this witness is a black man.

MICHAEL BROWN, JR.

The "Gentle Giant," as he is referred to by his mother and assorted family members just may not be so.

On the morning of August 9th, 2014 Michael and his latest, best good buddy, Dorian Johnson entered the Ferguson Food Market. Whilst there the big guy, Mike Brown Jr., who weights in at somewhere around 300 pounds and stands an imposing and towering six feet, four inches, purloined a stash of Cigarillos. In the process of obtaining the smokes, Brown slapped the clerk's hand away as he tried to reacquire the goods.

Several words exchanged, Brown and Johnson headed toward the front door.

The clerk, much smaller and middle aged, certainly no match for Brown Jr. Probably not even a good match for Dorian. The clerk attempted to detain the duo as they left the small store. Brown Jr. would have none of the clerk's admonishments to stop and return the goods. Nor would he stop as the clerk attempted to intersect him at the door. Brown Jr. shoved and pushed the clerk into a potato chip rack near the exit point.

After dealing with the vain attempts to stop the duo, both he and Johnson departed the area.

All activities within the Ferguson Food market are captured on the stores in house video system.

After leaving the store Brown Jr. and Adrian Johnson began walking toward their residence, located within the canfield Green Apartments.

They took the most direct route eventually ending up walking in the middle of the street on Canfield Dr.

Ferguson police officer Darren Wilson had just finished a radio call for a sick child. As Wilson proceeded on Canfield Dr. he observed two

18

subjects walking in the middle of the street.

Wilson slowed his marked police unit, a Chevrolet Tahoe, and request-ed that the pedestrians use the sidewalk. Wilson stated he said, "Hey guy what's wrong with the sidewalk." A normal request since the two impeded the normal flow of traffic. Cars were having difficulty navigating the thor-oughfare due to the obstruction caused by the two walkers.

Dorian Johnson said Wilson stated, "Get the fuck on the sidewalk."

Michael Brown Jr. then advised, "Fuck what you have to say."

Wilson then backed up his police car and advised his dispatcher, "I'll be out with two, send me another car." The result being that Michael Brown Jr., killed after he attacked the officer and attempted to gain con-trol of his weapon.

It is clear that an altercation took place at and within the police vehicle. What happened is explained by ballistics, DNA, witness testimony and the laws of physics.

As the reader will see later, medical professionals indicate in written reports and grand jury testimony that Michael Brown Jr., at the time of his death, was impaired.

In the event an individual wants to attract the attention of police an excellent way to accomplish that is to perpetrate a robbery, walk down the middle of the street causing vehicular traffic to veer around them and to engage in a physical confrontation with a police officer.

His mother, Leslie McSpadden, said her son "Was not a violent person."

Maybe not prior to that day. Maybe, who knows? Perhaps with his de-gree of impairment, which exceeded the bound by which a person thinks and acts rationally, Michael Brown Jr. did not consider the consequences of his actions. Maybe he wanted to get arrested.

Friends and acquaintances who lived near Michael like to point out that he finished high school. No small feat for this area. His friends were correct. The city of St. Louis has a 45.9% graduation rate. Can the Ferguson-Florissant School District be much better? An educated guess would be a resounding NO. Michael Brown Jr. jumped through some hoops in order to get his high school diploma. What happened after that?

He enrolled in the Vatterott College HVAC program and had a report date the following Monday. What happened?

Did Michael Brown Jr. feel comfortable in his current surroundings? Perhaps the task of getting up and traveling to nearby Berkley, MO to attend classes overwhelmed the lad.

Did he not receive counsel and guidance from his mother and father? The smallest bit of direction? The weight of becoming a productive member of society hanging heavy on his shoulders? Leaving the gang life and all the negative influences as well as the adverse effect on ones thought process.

Did the lack of a role model, parental guidance and mentoring by members of the community influence Michael? These valuable and productive assets are missing from many of the kids in and around the Canfield Green Apartments.

Michael grew up in a predominately one parent household. Children born into the environment of a one parent household are usually, but not always, the mother. The child or children as the case may be often shuffled off to the grandmother or other family members. Grandmothers often try, in vain, to rein in the teenagers. Many times to no effect. Kids are often left to their own devices. Soon, a number of the unsupervised kids come under the spell or control of gangs or other wayward youths. What good can come of activities spawned by a bunch of restless and energetic kids? Not much.

One could wonder. Did Michael's father ever take him and a few friends to a cardinal baseball game. Shoot hoops, play chess or any other activity with Michael and his friends?

Left to the "song of the streets" it wasn't long before Michael Brown Jr. immersed himself in the culture of the community. That of drinking, drug use and the criminality associated with those activities.

Dorian Johnson stated in his grand jury testimony that he acted in the capacity of a mentor to Michael Brown Jr. Why? Because Dorian, briefly exposed to college life at Lincoln University in Jefferson City, Missouri thought he could lend some of his knowledge of the university process to Michael. Brief indeed. Dorian spent less than a semester at this institution of higher learning. After leaving the halls of knowledge Dorian bounced around from job to job. The day Michael had the fateful confrontation with Ferguson police officer Darren Wilson, Dorian would, after a few marijuana laced Cigarillos, attempt to find gainful employment.

Gentle giant or thug, bully and criminal. Michael Brown Jr. had every avenue open. He may have successfully completed the HVAC program. He may have been successful at any number of endeavors. This is a path chosen by Mr. Brown. He had all the instrumentalities to become anything. He chose the wrong track.

The actions of Michael Brown Jr. on that tragic day caused his death. Michael Brown Jr did not have to die.

Gentle giant or criminal? Draw your own conclusion.

DORIAN JOHNSON

Dorian Johnson is Big Mike's accomplice in the initial robbery at the Ferguson Market and the confrontation with Officer Wilson.

Dorian wakes up around 7:00 AM on that fateful day. He asks his girlfriend if she wants some breakfast. Upon attending to his normal morning duties, he leaves to get breakfast items for his family.

Upon exiting the building, he bumps into Big Mike. They discuss "matching" each other for a blunt—exchanging a Cigarillo or 'rillo" laced with marijuana

Both men proceed to the Ferguson Market located at 9101 West Florissant Avenue, where Big Mike forcibly takes a quantity of Cigarillos and leaves the store. The store's surveillance system captures Brown pushing and shoving the store clerk, a man much smaller than Big Mike.

Officer Darren Wilson, westbound on Canfield Drive, observes the two men walking in the middle of the street. He tells them to get on the sidewalk and proceeds westbound.

Wilson then recalls the broadcast of the suspects wanted in the strong-arm robbery. He backs up his marked police Tahoe and attempts to detain Big Mike and Johnson. As events unfold, Michael Brown, Jr. attacks the officer, who subsequently shoots and kills him. Actions and activities of the incident vary widely. Upon completion of the investigation and taking into consideration all physical and forensic evidence, in addition to accounts by other witnesses who did not exaggerate or distort the facts, a true picture evolves.

In a televised statement to St. Louis media outlets, Johnson said:

> We was walking. We didn't have no weapons at all. We
> just having a conversation. No cars were blowing at us like we
> was holding up traffic or anything like that. A police officer

squad car pulls up and the officer says, "Get the F-up on the sidewalk."

We told the officer we wasn't but a minute away from our destination. We shortly be off the street, we be having a conversation, so he went up about his way, one or two seconds. Then he backs up and blocks both lanes, the way he turns his car. So he pulls up on the side of us and he tries to thrust his door open, but we was so close that it ricochets off of us and it bounces back to him. And I guess that gets him a little upset. At that time, he reaches out the window—he didn't get out the car. He grabs my friend around his neck, he was trying to choke my friend. He was trying to get away. The officer was trying to pull him into the car. At no time did the officer say anything. His weapon was drawn. He said, "I gonna shoot you," or "I'm gonna shoot," about the same moment the first shot went off. When we look down, Big Mike was shot, there was blood comin' from him. And we takes off runnin' and I hides by the first car I sees. Big Mike keeps runnin'. Once the officer gets outta the car and pursues my friend with drawn weapon. Now the officer didn't see any weapons drawn at him. He shoots again, and my friend feels that shot. He turnt around and puts his hands in the air and starts to get down but the officer still approaches with his weapon drawn. Then he fires several more shots and my friend dies. Didn't say anything to him, just stands over him shooting. I was so afraid that I just got up and ran.

Johnson also repeats this story for CNN.

Based on Johnson's statement, this appears to be a homicide by a police officer on a subject who was merely walking down the street.

Social media takes over—tweets and Facebook messages to friends and acquaintances of the electronic media. Everything, as is the current vernacular, "Went Viral."

Each message gets more detailed. A police officer shoots an unarmed kid. "Stands over him and shoots him in the back!"

"Comes out of the police car shooting."

"The kid had his hands up."

"The cop tries to strangle the kid, then he was shot ... for no damn reason."

So it went. Every communication filled with "eyewitness" who said ...

The already tense crowd dials it up several notches. Attempting to push their way into the crime scene, they fire shots into the air. Automatic weapon fire is heard from the interior of the increasingly angry crowd.

The sleepy and previously peaceful city of Ferguson would soon become the lead story for local, national, and international broadcast media.

Dorian gets his chance to express his "eyewitness" account of the incident on national and local media.

Ferguson is no longer a peaceful, sleepy town.

Game on.

TIFFANY AND PIAGET

According to the initial TV interviews and assorted tweets by Tiffany Mitchell and Piaget Crenshaw, "Michael Brown had his hands up ... and the officer just kept shooting."

These two eyewitnesses and Dorian Johnson also claimed that Brown "was running away, with his hands up and the officer just kept shooting."

These statements would lead one to believe that Mr. Brown received one or more rounds in the back.

Ms. Mitchell claims, "Wilson was trying to pull him into the car after the shot went off. Brown runs after about twenty feet, then jerks his body, as if he's been hit."

Ms. Crenshaw tells anyone who would listen, "I saw the police chase him down the street and shoot him down."

Add these statement to the initial interview of Dorian Johnson and the net result is a bubbling caldron of misinformation fueled by the constant, incorrect, and inflammatory tweets and Facebook posts by subjects not at the scene of the incident or even in the state of Missouri.

The "hands up" story is totally false, but one thing is locked in the minds of those that want to believe. It is true in the minds of millions of people throughout the country, thanks, in large part, to a media eager for a race controversy. Our president and attorney general didn't help matters when they could and should have assisted with truthful and honest words about what really happened.

COMETH NOW, JAY, AH … UM, NIXON, GOVERNOR OF THE GREAT STATE OF MISSOURI

The governor of the great state of Missouri, Jay Nixon, is a man with an agenda. That agenda is to be on Hillary's ticket. Shooting for the vice-president slot, Hillary would want a strong leader on the VP position. A strong leader, a democrat from the Midwest, one to balance the ticket and perhaps turn a few red states blue? Certainly Missouri.

A what? A shooting in Ferguson? A white cop, a black man-child killed by an overbearing, racist white cop. Ah ha, the perfect opportunity to show the democrat establishment what the governor is made of.

I'll just appoint a black guy from the Highway Patrol. A fine law enforcement entity, if your main purpose is to write traffic tickets and work accidents. A fine law enforcement organization indeed. Urban policing—not so much.

Let's see, a black guy. A black guy in a command position. Why Captain Ron Johnson, the commander of Troop "C"—the troop responsible for St. Louis county and 11 surrounding counties in east central Missouri.

Ron Johnson, a fine man and by all accounts, an efficient and effective communicator and administrator. Like the good soldier when ordered to conduct a task, he salutes and moves out smartly.

After several nights of rioting, taunting the police, and burning businesses along the west Florissant Road corridor in the cities of Jennings, Ferguson, and Dellwood, Missouri, Ron Johnson takes his post as the site commander.

Initial success with the protesters is soon followed by the appearance of the Guy Fawkes masks and agitators from Washington, California, and the four corners of the United States.

Two additional police shootings in the city of St. Louis add nothing but high-grade aviation fuel to an already tense situation. Has the St. Louis metro area become the epicenter for police shootings? More importantly, have thugs become emboldened and feel that police officers have lost the ability to protect themselves or other citizens?

On his first day/night as the operational commander, he orders all officer to remove gas masks and protective gear.

Chief Jon Belmar becomes irate and orders the St. Louis county officers to remain in full, protective gear, a bold and gutsy move that furthers his persona as a resolute and forceful leader. County police officers face off with a crowd of protesters that are growing more hostile on a daily basis. The uniform, helmets', shin guards, and protective vests offend the peaceful protesters, who declare, "They scare us."

Several highway patrol troopers approach the county officers and asked them to stay close. "You see, we don't have any protective gear." Some troopers worked the line in their campaign hats. A long-standing tradition with the troopers. Looks great, gentlemen, wonder what would happen if that hat met a brick or a water bottle full of ice.

Soon after the "hug-a-thug" mentality vanishes and all officers on the line are fully attired in riot gear.

Okay, things are kinda under control. The governor calls a press conference. To show his openness and his standard of inclusion, he opens it to all. However, these political folks aren't familiar with urban policing or activities. Many people feel that a press conference consists of who can interrupt the most, in the loudest tone. Over-talking, in the world of some peaceful protesters, is considered an Olympic event.

This is unlike the gracious and sanitized press conferences the governor is used to. One softball question after another. Grandiose and patronizing answers. A lot of smiling and backslapping—or maybe backstabbing.

" ... In Ferguson, people of all races and creeds are joining hands to pray for justice. But we will not be defeated by bricks and guns and Molotov cocktails. With the help of peaceful demonstrators, Captain Johnson and law enforcement will not give up trying to ensure that those with peace in their hearts are not drowned out by those with senseless violence in their hands."

"Second, a vigorous prosecution (of officer Darren Wilson) must now be pursued …"

A **vigorous prosecution?** The governor is a lawyer. He must know that before a vigorous prosecution can be undertaken, a vigorous **investigation** must be conducted. Just where did this guy go to law school? Bob's law school and liquors?

Wonder what the Democratic organization thinks of this guy now?

A reporter asks, "You're the sitting governor. Nine days into the investigation, you called for a vigorous prosecution. You don't think in any way that undermined the grand jury process?"

Governor Jay Nixon responds, "My … uh … As I said many times, folks concerning that … um … what I meant when I said that was the whole entire process of investigation and … uh … next question."

"The democratically elected St. Louis county prosecutor and the attorney general of the United States each have a job to do."

But wait, there's more.

November 11, 2014, the governor calls a press conference before the announcement of the St. Louis county grand jury sitting in the matter of the State of Missouri vs. Darren Wilson.

The grand jury decision is expected at any time. The governor wanted to ensure the citizens of his strong and resolute determination to keep people safe while allowing protesters to express their grievances.

About halfway into the press circus, Chief Jon Belmar steps to the microphone to address a question the governor handed off with a number of ah … um … ah … um's.

Chief Belmar answers all questions without stumbling. A polished and astute police chief, Belmar handles questions like former Cardinal Ozzie Smith used to field red-hot baseballs at Busch Stadium.

Later, the governor calls yet another news conference, this one a phone conference with reporters. Asked if it was his ultimate responsibility how any protests are policed, he said, "We're, … um … you know, our goal here is to, is to keep the peace and allow folks' voices to be heard. And in that balance, attempting, you know, I am, using the resources we have to be predictable … I don't spend a tremendous amount of time personalizing this, vis-a-vis me."

What?

"I prefer not to be a commentator on it. I'm making decisions, as, in a, you know, to make sure we are prepared for all contingencies," he added.

Asked again if any one official or agency is ultimately in charge in terms of a response, he said, "Well, I mean, it clearly, I mean, I, I feel good about the—we worked hard to establish unified command, allied responsibilities, and now the additional assets provided by my order today, with the national guard, you know—we have worked through a number of operational issues."

Huh?

Can this guy string a sentence together? Probably not. Maybe he should have kept his nose out of the issue and let law enforcement handle the protests. Chief Belmar and the commanders of the St. Louis county police department along with the Missouri highway patrol and other law enforcement agencies could have handled the situation without the governor. His comments and attempted statements about the issue only confused and baffled citizens. Citizens that deserve better.

CAN YOU FEEL THE LOVE?

On October 18, 2014, Perarlie Gordon, the mother-in law of Michael Brown, Sr. sets up a tent at 9300 West Florissant—this is the business that housed Red's B-B-Q. From the tent, she and several members of her family sell "Justice for Mike Brown" T-shirts and afghans.

At 1:30 p.m., about 20 subjects accost Ms. Gordon and her entourage. Michael Brown, Jr.'s mother, Leslie McSpadden, advises Ms. Gordon, "You can't sell this shit."

Ms. Gordon responds by saying that unless McSpadden could produce documentation stating she has a patent on her son's name, she would continue to sell her merchandise.

Desureia Harris, Michael Brown, Jr.'s grandmother says, "You don't know my grandson like that. I'm gonna tear this shit down."

Several interlopers repeatedly strike Ms. Gordon on the back. Ms. Gordon went on to advise the officers of the Ferguson police department there were 20 to 30 unknown subjects tearing down her booth. In the affray, Ms. Gordon falls to the asphalt.

Gordon heard McSpadden say, "That's Caluina's mom, get her ass!" Ms. Gordon is the mother of Michael Brown, Sr.'s current girlfriend.

During the altercation, the rapscallions take over $1,500.00 in merchandise and a suitcase containing about $400.00 in cash.

Several relatives and friends of Ms. Gordon are treated for injuries at the scene. One, transported to a local hospital, has yet to give a statement.

The confrontation, witnessed by a person stopped at a traffic light nearby, confirms the story relayed by Ms. Gordon.

Lack of cooperation by the victims and witnesses closes the case, a disposition not unlike many other cases involving family, instant rage, and money.

Once again ... can ya feel the love?

State of Missouri v. Darren Wilson

Grand Jury Volume I

August 20, 2014

The following is a transcript of the grand jury proceedings, at the offices of St. Louis County Prosecuting Attorney's Office, 100 South Central Avenue, in the City of Clayton, State of Missouri, on the 20th day of August, 2014.

FOR THE STATE: MR ROBERT McCULLOCH

MS SHELIA WHIRLEY

MS KATHI ALIZADEH

INTRODUCTION

MR. McCULLOCH:

Thank you. For the record, I'm Bob McCulloch, the prosecutor. I want to talk to you a little bit about this. As you are well aware, we are here about the shooting death of Michael Brown.

I want to tell you how this is going to proceed. Obviously, it is going to be different from a lot of the other cases that you've heard during your term on this grand jury.

First things first. I know a lot of you already know these two ladies, but for the record, let me introduce Kathi Alizadeh and Shelia Whirley. They will be the primary, if not the exclusive attorneys, working in the grand jury on this case.

Obviously, I hope many other people will be working on things outside of us getting this case ready for the presentation that Kathi and/or Sheila will make.

Kathi is the prosecutor I have on call for the month of August for all homicide calls, so she received the call about this shooting within minutes of the time the Ferguson police notified the county police. She has been working with the police and handling lots of other things on this since the beginning.

My procedure is always that I have a prosecutor on call solely for the purpose of handling homicide cases from start to finish.

Shelia, as you know, has been assigned to the grand jury term, so she will continue with this grand jury on the Brown case for as long as it takes.

I want to go over a few things. First and foremost, I wish to tell you that this is the first, last, and probably the only time I think that you will see me in relation to this case—certainly in the grand jury. The court reporter, who is under the same oath essentially as are all witnesses, will record everything that you and I do.

As I said, Kathi and Shelia will be the primary attorneys, the attorneys responsible for presenting everything to the grand jury.

I'm going to go over just a few things to make sure that I cover the ground rules for the procedure.

As you know, your term ends on the 10th of September and you also have dockets. No dockets are next week, but are scheduled for the 3rd and 10th. Those dockets may be adjusted, but will not be cancelled.

Since this case is still in the middle of an ongoing investigation, noticeable activity will occur. I am certain you are well aware of what's happening during the day—even out in front of the courthouse here on several occasions—and during the evening in your homes.

In addition, the federal government and the department of justice are doing a parallel, but independent investigation of the same thing.

As that is going back and forth, the county police will be re-interviewing some witnesses that haven't or won't talk. We're giving them all statements and any other information that we have on this matter.

So after September 10th, your term is extended, and the only matter that you will hear anything on will be this Michael Brown case, the Michael Brown shooting. You won't have the docket because another grand jury that starts the following week will be reviewing what you have been doing for the past four months.

By the way, we greatly appreciate your service on that. You have done a great job for the people of this county.

Obviously, we want to be as expeditious as possible, but not rush through this case. If that means meeting for hours every day—Saturdays, evenings—whatever works is what we are going to do, as long as it works for everybody's schedule, and as long as you get it. If all twelve of you have an entire day, we will have an entire day.

Everything will be recorded. Starting with the oath by the court reporter and everything that I'm saying now and everything that anybody says, whether that person is a witness, one of the attorneys, or one of the jurors, it will be recorded.

I wish to remind you that unlike a trial jury, the questions, you have been discussing and what you've heard perhaps between witnesses or during breaks and the like—that's part of your deliberation. However, none of that happens while anybody else is in the room and that includes the attorney and court reporter.

At the end of each witness testimony, the reporter will make an announcement that essentially indicates he is going to finalize the disc. For every witness who testifies and for each session of that testimony, the recorder makes a separate disc, so that when he finalizes that, it finalizes the disc.

After that, the disc cannot be altered—nothing can be added, nothing can be deleted. If the same witness comes back at some other time, we make a separate disc for the second testimony and we will do the same for every person who comes in and testifies.

Every bit of the evidence from the photos, the scene of the shooting and diagrams, the physical evidence that was seized at that time at the location, the DNA evidence—anything and everything that pertains to this case will be presented to the grand jury. It will be available to you for your review as it is coming in.

Shelia, primarily, will be at least getting things started in terms of asking the witness questions, much as you've seen her doing for the whole summer.

You're experienced enough now that you can ask whatever questions you want to ask of jurors. Any item, anything you want to ask any witness, absolutely ask for that information.

Let me back up a little on the topic of questions, while we are talking about the records on that issue.

Just remember that it's going to take a few minutes for the technicians to finalize this disc once the testifying witness is finished. So if you have discussion or you want to talk or ask each other questions—anything at all like that—make sure you wait long enough until finalization is complete and everyone else has left.

The technical team will stick around long enough to remind you of that, so please wait until everybody else is gone before you talk about anything related to this case, because that's not something that anyone but the jurors should hear.

If you have a question about what a witness said or what is happening, those questions must wait until the witness comes back to answer them in person.

The judge talked to you this morning about your oath, which is very similar to one each witness will take. Remember that these are confidential proceedings, so nothing leaves this room unless ordered by the court or by some other legal method. I will talk about those in just a second.

In addition to matters of confidentiality and your oath, is one of anonymity. You are anonymous. You are protected by law—your names and addresses are not public—no information about you is public.

Concerning the demographics of any publicity, some information may come public in terms of age, race, or gender.

I just want to share that you're protected by law—that's been litigated—personal information such as your names will not be released.

However, the media kind of comes and goes around here. I did a number of interviews with local people today for a couple of reasons, just to get it all out of the way, so we're finished with that.

I can't control whether someone shows up outside the doors and just hangs around. If a protest is scheduled or the media is going to be here, we will work with that as needed.

The only other thing I'd say is when you are coming in, don't wear your grand jury badge, so as not to tip anybody off that you are on the jury.

Regarding taking notes, you may take all the notes you want. Write down anything and everything. If a thought occurs to you or you need to talk to a witness, take all the notes you want. The notes, of course, can't leave here. However, these are your notes and your notes alone. Fellow grand jurors won't see your notes and you won't see theirs. At the end of day or end of session, we will collect the notes and secure them, as well as any evidence. We have highly secure evidence lockers within the complex here.

Afterwards, you can use your notes for any deliberations when everything is finished. Just so you know, massive amounts of information and physical items will be coming in here in the next month. You're not going to remember everything. After the witness today testifies, you're not going to remember that a month from now, but all of that and the transcripts will be available and you'll have as long as need, as long as you want, to go through everything again before you start your deliberations.

Unlike a jury trial where you have to send a note to the judge, who decides if you are allowed to have something, that rule doesn't apply here. Everything will be here in the room with you and you will have access to all of it, including your notes throughout your term on this grand jury.

You must keep an open mind on everything. You haven't heard a single thing yet, other than what is being said in the media, and believe me, that's not evidence. Don't form any opinion on anything that you've heard, good, bad, or ugly in the media.

Everything that's been collected, every statement that has ever been made, will be available to you. You need to keep an open mind to give everybody, including the entire community, as full and open-minded opinion as you can, but certainly be as thorough as you can, while making as expedient a review of all the evidence that is possible.

At the end of all this, I know people keep talking about transparency, which depends on your ability to determine if there are charges you find should be lodged. All that information will come out pursuant to the course of this case. Certain rules that apply as to how things are handled, but that doesn't come out right away, because you can't prejudice a potential jury panel. So we present all that evidence, just like here, to a trial jury in the courtroom—not to the media—so everybody can see it and make their minds up before they ever come into a courtroom.

If you determine no charges are to be filed, then everything will be released immediately or as close to immediately as we can get. Every bit of evidence you have—the testimony of the witnesses who came in, the statements of those witnesses, the physical evidence, the photographs— everything that you have seen and heard will be released to the public. That is as transparent as we can get, short of putting a pool of TV cameras in here. However, that's not going to happen.

The most important thing is that you obtain all the information and evidence you need and then make your determination.

Thank you for your service to this county and to your fellow citizens. This is probably the last time you will see me, so thanks for your undivided attention to these matters.

State of Missouri v. Darren Wilson

Grand Jury Volume IV

September 10, 2014

Excerpts from the grand jury testimony of Dorian Johnson: This testimony was provided after Dorian Johnson gave interviews to St. Louis media outlets, MSNBC, and CNN shortly after the Michael Brown shooting.

FOR THE STATE: MS WHIRLEY
                   MS ALIZADEH

EXAMINATION

MS WHIRLEY:

Q.   All right. Let's talk—you knew Mike Brown, right? You call him Big Mike? Can I refer to him as Big Mike?

A.   Absolutely, I will call him Big Mike, too, if you don't mind.

Q.   So you were good friends with Big Mike?

A.   We were friends, but not childhood friends.

Q.   Tell us how you met Big Mike.

A.   I only been staying in these here apartments for about eight months. I met Big Mike around the fifth month I was living there. I met him through a friend I knows from the area, who lives down the street.

       This here friend introduced Big Mike when they came to my place one day. They wants to play video games, you know, relax and have conversation—I didn't have no problem with that.

Q.   Did you socialize with him on a regular basis after that or how often would you say you were with him?

A.   Like I says, it was my apartment, so you know, I had bills and things like that. I was working at the time of me first moving into the apartments. I just lost my job around the sixth month, I met him the fifth month, so now I'm just about to find work and a new way to pay the bills, so I didn't have no time to connect with him every day or even every week, 'cause I was trying to find work.

Q.   When you met him, and on August 9th at the time of the shooting, was he living in North Winds?

A.   No, he just moved out of his gramma's house and was staying with this friend.

Q. But you really didn't hang out with him?

A. No, ma'am, not on a daily basis.

Q. You were a few years older?

A. Yeah.

Q. Okay. Had you ever been to his grandmother's house?

A. One time. At that time I think his gramma was real strict on who she let inside her home.

Q. Okay, so we're going to be talking a lot about August 9th—you realize that?

A. Yes, ma'am.

Q. On the day of the shooting, August the 9th, tell us how your day began.

A. August the 9th, it began like any other day. Upon getting some breakfast, I git me some 'rillos. I smokes mornings when I start my day off, so's I was headed to the store.

Q. Now wait a minute—just stop here to make sure we're all clear. So that is kind of what generally happens for you in the morning?

A. In the morning, yeah.

Q. You got up around 7:00 on August 9th?

A. Around 7 that morning.

Q. Tell us what happened after you got up.

A. When I got up and got dressed or whatnot, I go outta my front door. I see Big Mike across the parking lot.

Q. Okay. And what—did you go over to where he was or did he come to you?

A. Yeah, just coincidently, the guy I was going to see lived on the path. Big Mike was outside and alone at the time. He told me he was staying with a friend, the one that I knew, and he was upstairs asleep.

Q. And did you and Mike, based on information I've heard, did you guys kind of hook up at that point that morning?

A. Yeah, when I sees him, I stops and speaks to him. He asked me where I was headed to. I told him, I was going to get some 'rillos and something to eat. He was like, "Okay, well, I'll match you." I guess he had his

39

own weed, so he said he would match me one. Matching is, if you don't know, I roll the weed, he roll the blunt, and we both exchange blunts.

Q.   In matching, does that mean that one person has the weed and one person has the 'rillos?

A.   Both smokers has weed and 'rillos, so they just be smoking together.

Q.   So he said he would match you?

A.   Correct.

Q.   Had you all smoked, matched, and smoked yet?

A.   Not yet, no.

Q.   You said there was a person in the complex that actually sold 'rillos?

A.   Yes.

Q.   Is that where you were heading?

A.   Yeah.

Q.   But that changed?

A.   Yes, it did.

Q.   Tell us how.

A.   Big Mike, he was telling me he was about to go off to school. I was telling him about my past experience in school. When I graduated high school, I went straight on to Lincoln University. So I was telling him some of the challenges that he was gonna face, even though it weren't a university, he was gonna face some challenges. Basically, our conversation was about the future.

Q.   Okay.

A.   It kinda took my mind off the person in the complex. When I told him I was gonna get 'rillos, he was like, I need that too. Let's walk to the store. By that time, the conversation was so deep I forgot about the person I was gonna see, so we just ended up walking to the store.

Q.   So from the time you left Canfield Green, you saw Big Mike and talked to him, and then went to the market?

A.   Correct.

Q.   So tell us about the market—what happened at the market?

A.   Before walking to the store, it never came up that Big Mike didn't have no money. I had money, I had money in my pocket. We was gonna buy 'rillos, in my mind that's what we were gonna do.

Q.   Okay.

A.   When we got to the store, Big Mike talks to the store clerk eye-to-eye, face-to-face. I'm standing right behind Big Mike.

Q.   Is it a female or male store clerk?

A.   It's a man he's talking to. I also sees the girl clerk, she's at her register and she is just looking at us.

Q.   But he is talking to the male store clerk?

A.   Yes, he is.

Q.   Go ahead.

A.   As he is talking to the clerk, the guy ask him what does he want. Big Mike says in a very not, you know, threatening voice, he just said what he wanted—a box of 'rillos. While he was saying it, he was leaning forward to grab them.

Q.   Okay.

A.   That was when he pulls back and he hands me the box—it was a box of mini 'rillos. He turns around to gimme 'em.

Q.   Okay.

A.   It wasn't until the second time when he grabs a handful of the single 'rillos. As he was coming back, the clerk did a late response and swung his hand, but missed, 'cause he was so late, and he smacked the counter.

Q.   The store clerk did?

A.   Yes.

Q.   I see.

A.   The clerk was in front of the register, I was standing right behind him. The guy kinda hit the top of some 'rillos, so they be fallin' all over. And Big Mike turns to pick 'em up, but as he picks those up, he faces to-wards the door. That's when I knew okay, something is not right here.

Q.   Okay.

A.   Because I'm standing behind him, but I'm trying to pick up some of the 'rillos, I'm athinkin', am I being pranked or is this something? I was trying to gather that in my head at the time. Now while all of this is goin' on, Big Mike is making his way towards the door. The clerk come around his register and he's making his way to the door. Big Mike's almost at the door, so he was gonna put his hand on the door, to, you know, push the door open.

By that time, the clerk was almost in front of the door, but he didn't get there right directly in front of the door, so much as put his hand on it.

Big Mike, he thrust the door open to where the door slips outta the clerk's hand, so the door flew open. By that time, I knew—I saw what was goin' on, but I didn't know it was going to happen that way. So I was trying to pull myself as far away from any contact as fast as possible, 'cause I didn't know what was gonna happen.

So at that time he slung the door open, I was making my way around Big Mike and the store clerk so's I could exit the store, 'cause I didn't want any part of it—I knows there be cameras in the store.

When Big Mike tries to go out and thrust the door open, it comes outta the clerk's hand. He tries to grab, like it was a very fast motion, but the he never came off of neither one of his feet. He never fell on the floor or got punched or anything like that, it was just a very fast motion—just a shove.

Q. Okay. What did you guys do then?

A. Big Mike didn't so much as give me an answer as to why he did it, 'cause he was basically laughing his head off, saying, "Be cool, be calm,"—stuff like that, laughing it off, but in my head, I'm like, *I can't be calm, I can't be cool, 'cause I know what just happened and we was on camera!*

Q. Did he seem like he had smoked some marijuana or something before you saw him that morning?

A. Yeah, based on what I saw of him that morning before we walked to the store.

Q. Okay, so you guys are walking towards West Florissant?

A. We was walking down West Florissant, from Ferguson Market to Canfield Green.

Q. Are you running or hiding?

A. No.

Q. You walk to West Florissant and then what street takes you in to Canfield?

A. Canfield Drive.

Q. So you walk up Canfield Drive?

A. Well, once we get to Canfield, I sees another police cruiser passes us by. Now this one, I believe, in my mind, he was going to the store. But we gets to Canfield and now we're walking down Canfield.

Q. Are a lot of cars out on Canfield, out at this time, a lot of traffic?

A. At that time, no.

Q. Okay, okay. So now you are walking, I guess, east on Canfield?

A. Yes, ma'am.

Q. All right. Tell us what happens?

A. At that time, there's no cars, no traffic, no one coming up or down Canfield Drive. We gets in the middle of the street …

Q. Let me ask you a question. Where were you guys headed at this point?

A. We was headed back to my house.

Q. Okay. And your plan was to go and smoke?

A. Yeah, smoke, something like that.

Q. Okay. Go ahead and finish.

A. As we was walkin' down the street, I sees the police cruiser approaching us, comin' up. When he gets right directly on the side of us, the police officer, Darren Wilson, rolls down his window and says, "Get on the sidewalk,"—says it very rudely.

Q. You can say exactly whatever he said.

A. He said, "Get the fuck on the sidewalk!"

Q. Had you ever had any interaction with Officer Wilson before?

A. No, ma'am.

Q. Nobody said, "Oh, I know him"?

A. Nope, nobody said anything like that—it was just Big Mike an' me. Now at that time I was looking at the officer's face, but not really in his eyes. I was the one talking to the officer and I wasn't loud or anything. I was just telling him where we was headed.

Q. How close were you and Big Mike at that time?

A. He's like right on my back.

Q. All right. Go ahead.

A. So we continued to walk. In my mind, I thought he was just thinkin', you know, *Okay they're just kids, they will get out of the street shortly.*

Q. Okay.

A. We continued to walk and have our conversation, but almost a split second later, we hears tires screeching, and the officer, he pulls back in traffic real fast, to the point of an angle. He reverses so fast on an angle that now we's almost inches away from his front door, like we was right in his face now.

Q. Okay, so both of you are facing the driver's side door?

A. The driver's side door.

Q. Okay, all right. Go ahead—so you all are at the door and then what?

A. The officer pulls back and says very loud and angry, "What did you say?"

Q. Who did the officer appear to be talking to?

A. At the time, I believe he was talking to both of us. Like I said, Big Mike never said anything when the officer pulls up on us. The instant Big Mike finishes saying something, the officer thrust his door open real hard. We was so close to the door it hit mostly Big Mike, but it hit me on my left side and it closed real fast. Just the same speed, boom, boom— that fast.

And at that time, he never tried to open the door again or tries to git back out, but his arm came outta the window and that's the first initial contact they had. The officer grabbed ahold of Big Mike's shirt around the neck.

Q. Was there any warning, did Officer Wilson just stick his hand out and grab or did he say anything?

A. No, ma'am, at this time when the door was closed back on him, he didn't say nothin'. His arm almost in an instant came outta the window, his left arm, I remember, that came outta the window and grabs Big Mike around his neck area and his throat. I watch his hands—you know, they really tighten up, so yeah, he had a good grip on him, that what I first seen.

Q.   Were you still right behind Big Mike when this occurred?

A.   I weren't behind him no more. We're side by side, so I sees all what's goin' on. Now from the beginning of the grab, it's a tug of war. Big Mike places one hand openly on top of the cruiser and the other hand more right up under the window, the side mirror, trying to pull off the officer's grip.

Q.   How is he doing that with the Cigarillos in his hand?

A.   He keeps the 'rillos in his hand as he puts his hands on the car. He never drops a single pack. He still has them in his hand not dropping them, but pulling away, but he still grab on to 'em. So he never could really get a good grip on the car, but he's really trying to pull away.

Q.   Okay.

A.   At this time, I'm not hearing what the officer is saying and I'm not hearing what Big Mike is saying. So now I'm not in shock—that's the beginning of my shock level. That's where I'm like, *This doesn't happen every day, something is out of order here.* They were both very upset and they couldn't calm down. There wasn't any wrestling or anything like that, no punches were thrown.

Q.   Okay. So please tell us what happened?

A.   And at that point, Big Mike turns to me, so now we's face-to-face, and he puts his hands like, "Grab these, bro." And in shock, my hands were open to where he could put the 'rillos in my hand, but I'm still standing in the same spot.

At that time, I couldn't open my mouth, couldn't speak. I wanted to say, "Could someone calm down." And the 'rillos was placed in my hand. At that time, Big Mike turns around, facing the officer now, so he could get a good grip on the car.

So now he's pulling away, it's with more power, with more force. The officer is trying to pull him inside the vehicle through the window, like he's pulling him, but Big Mike, he's pulling away. The officer never attempts to open his door again. Now he's trying to pull him, but Big Mike's pulling away.

Q.   Was he pulling him with both his hands?

A.   No.

Q.   The officer is only using his left hand?

A.   The officer is only using his left hand, trying to pull Big Mike in. I could tell Big Mike was getting the best of the officer, because he was in a better position. Officer Wilson looked strong enough to pull, but not strong enough to pull him all the way in the car.

       Now, in the midst of this tug of war, I never see Big Mike actually have his body inside the vehicle, 'cause the officer never fully got him inside, so much as he has torso or top area coming toward the window.

Q.   Did you ever see Big Mike's hands inside the car?

A.   No, ma'am, I never and I'm still standing there.

Juror Questions:

Ms. Whirley: Is there a question?

Juror: I do have a question.

Ms. Whirley: It's okay with me.

Juror: Do you want to wait?

Ms. Whirley: No, go ahead.

Juror: You said you were both on his right?

A.   Yes, ma'am.

Q.   You were both very close to the door?

A.   Yes, ma'am.

Q.   You said he had his hands on the police car?

A.   Correct.

Q.   And he handed you the Cigarillos in your hand?

A.   Yes, ma'am, correct.

Q.   Did he and you both have them in one hand?

A.   Correct, yes—no, he handed both of them in my hands. My hands were free, so he handed them to me at the same time.

Q.   The reason I ask this, I'm not judging, the reason I ask you is because in the film we saw, he only had Cigarillos in one hand.

A. Yes, when he initially grabbed 'em out of the store, he had a lot of them in one hand. Once he got outside the store, that's when he divided 'em kind of and had 'em in both of his hands.

Q. He's 6'3" or 6'4"?

A. Yes, ma'am.

Q. So how do you know, since he is so much taller than the car or you, that you saw both of his hands—how did you see his left hand?

A. He's so big and he's up against the car.

Q. How could you be so sure?

A. I see what you's saying, but he was never that close to the car. Like I said, because of the position Big Mike was standing outside, he was more overpowering the officer, who couldn't get him close to the car. I sees Big Mike's hands as he's pulling away, but the officer, you know, there's a tug of war, but Big Mike pulls away.

Q. That begs another question. You said he was getting the best of the officer. So was the car was moving, like was it so much force that it was rocking or something?

A. Yes, it was moving.

Q. Because Big Mike was getting the best of the officer?

A. Yes.

Q. If Big Mike is 300 pounds and 6'3", there has to be movement of the car?

A. Yeah, 'cause he was standing away from the car, it was moving.

Q. You had only met Mike, I think you said about three months before this incident occurred—is that correct?

A. One or two months.

Q. Okay. Now while you were there, I'm of the impression—I don't want to speculate—you had no other contact with the Ferguson police department for any reason, any tickets or any altercations or anything of that nature?

A. No, ma'am, I never had none.

Ms. Whirley: Did you have another question?

Juror: Yeah, I had another question. Was there any particular reason when the police officer gives you an order that you and Mike did not obey that order to get out of the street at that time and onto the sidewalk?

A.   The reason, I mean, at the time in my head and the response that I gave back to the officer, I didn't feel like I was rude. I knew by law that we wasn't committing a crime at the time—there was no traffic or nothin' like that, 'cause cars were still able to pass us.

So at that time, if the officer didn't know and I feel he didn't know about the store, 'cause Big Mike still was holding the 'rillos in his hands in plain sight of the officer when he pulled up on us. The officer was just saying to get on the sidewalk. Once I responded to him, telling him we was a minute away from our destination, I felt like that we wasn't committing a crime.

At that time, the officer really didn't look like, you know, that he was mad or that he was telling us that we was committing a crime—he was just saying we was to get on the sidewalk. We thought we was basically okay, since we was getting' outta the street in a minute.

Juror: Did you, I mean did the thought ever come to your mind at that point in time, that maybe he was doing it for public safety to avoid you being struck by a vehicle in the street—for your own safety?

A.   At the time, no, I didn't think so.

Q.   My question before we get started back is when the officer pulled back, did he ever question you about the store incident?

A.   No, ma'am.

Q.   And at that point, the altercation ensued?

A.   It started there.

Ms Alizadeh: Is it possible that Big Mike, who is behind you now, could have said something to the officer as he pulled away, that Big Mike could possibly have said something ignorant to him?

A.   No way, no, ma'am. Big Mike was standing behind me. He was so close if he said something like that, I would've heard. He didn't say nothin'— like I said at that time, I only talks to the officer.

Q.   Let's get back to the actual shooting.

A.   Okay.

Q.   We left off with you talking about the officer having his left hand out of the car, and he is pulling Big Mike in or trying to, so now the Cigarillos have been handed off to you?

A.   Yes, ma'am.

Q.   Go on from there.

A.   Big Mike and Darren Wilson, the officer, they are doing their tug of war. He passes off the 'rillos. Now he's back, but at no point in time did I begin to move away. I stood in the same position, same spot.

At that time, I was looking at Big Mike when the officer says, "I'll shoot." In my mind, I think, taser—I see people get tasered before and it looks like it hurts a lot.

Q.   Let me stop you a minute. So the first time the officer says, "I'll shoot," Big Mike's hands are free?

A.   Yeah.

Q.   He's given you the Cigarillos?

A.   Yes.

Q.   No shots have been fired yet?

A.   Not at the moment, no.

Q.   Okay, so when the officer is saying, "I'll shoot!" do you know where Big Mike's hands are?

A.   I can see both Officer Wilson's hands and Big Mike's.

Q.   Tell us about it.

A.   Big Mike's left hand was still on, like right above the mirror. His other arm now, 'cause of the tug of war pull, the officer's grip comes up, from up on his neck, to the shirt collar, to the shoulder, so basically he never lets go. Now he has Big Mike.

Q.   So the officer has his right arm?

A.   Yes, with his left arm, the officer's out the window grabbing Big Mike's right arm.

Q.   Okay. So he has Big Mike's right arm. Does he pull it inside the car?

A.   Once the officer said he would shoot, my focus switches and locks on the officer, 'cause in my mind, I assume it's a taser. But when I sees the gun and the barrel, I goes into a deep shock.

Q. You didn't think everybody should just stop when you saw the gun?

A. I was praying, I was. I was so victimized that people don't even understand. I felt victimized, 'cause I felt so afraid that I couldn't talk. I couldn't say what was on my mind, 'cause I was so afraid, I couldn't calm it down.

Q. Let's just go back. I understand what you are saying about seeing the shooting like that, but when Big Mike's right hand or arm is being pulled into the car—I don't know if you said that or not—you said that the officer had his right hand inside the cruiser, but his left hand had Big Mike's right arm?

A. Correct.

Q. Did you see it or not—where was Big Mike's right hand?

A. I didn't see Big Mike's right hand, because the officer had it, but his other hand was up, so there could've been times when the officer pulled Big Mike's right hand, 'cause his left hand never moved off the police car.

Q. So where were Big Mike's hands? I'm interested in the hands and the arms.

A. When the officer said he was gonna shoot, Big Mike's hand is not on the car anymore.

Q. That's the left hand?

A. The left arm is not on the car anymore, the officer still has the right arm, but Big Mike's not inside the car. And when I look up, I sees the officer has his gun pointed at Big Mike.

In my mind, it was probably aimed at both of us, but I guess he wasn't directly just trying to go for Big Mike. He had his gun pointed towards us. I'm still standing in the doorway and it looks like the officer was gonna say again he'd shoot, but he didn't get to finish his sentence—the gun just went off.

Q. At the time the gun went off, where were the hands of Big Mike?

A. The left arm was down at his side. He was standing straight up and I was standing next to him. His right arm was still up in the air, pulling off the car, and pulling the officer.

At this time, like I said, I see more of the officer's arm outside the car than Big Mike's arm inside the car, so he has a better position to pull away from the officer, who's sitting down.

Q. Just so I understand—with the officer's left hand, he's pulling Big Mike's right arm into the car. Big Mike's pulling away, while the officer still has his gun in his right hand?

A. Correct

Q. Is that when Officer Wilson says he is going to shoot?

A. Correct.

Ms. Whirley: While this pulling is going on?

A. Correct, yes, ma'am.

Q. Okay. Go ahead. Excuse me, is there a question?

Juror: Real quick, when the gun went off as soon as the officer said he would shoot, do you know if the gun was inside or outside the car?

A. The gun definitely was inside the car when the officer fired the shot. How me and Big Mike was standing, we was standing straight up, so we definitely is outside the vehicle. The bullet came outside the car and hit Big Mike. He was never inside the car—he was outside the car when the first shot went off. The officer was inside the car, so the gun was inside the car, but when he shot the gun, the bullet went outside the car and hit Big Mike in the chest—I seen the blood running.

Q. Ms. Whirley: You are not sure where the wound—

A. It struck him, I definitely know that it hit him, 'cause I saw the blood with the first shot.

Q. Are you absolutely certain? I know you talked about being in shock and that kind of thing, but this is *very* important. This jury is trying to get this thing figured out. Are you absolutely certain that you did not see Big Mike's hand inside the police car during the struggle with the officer?

A. Now I won't speculate on his hand being inside the car, like I said, 'cause there was times where the officer had a good pull and his arm would get in there, but most of the time the officer really didn't have that much power, 'cause of the position that they both had.

Q. Right, can you go ahead?

A. I never saw at no point in time Big Mike's hand touch the gun or anything like that, 'cause of the gun was already drawn.

Q.   How about touching the officer?

A.   Now, touching the officer—maybe, 'cause they're pulling each other, but as far as hitting the officer—no, I didn't see that.

Q.   You didn't ever see Big Mike make a fist?

A.   No, ma'am, he never had his fist clenched up like in a punching manner, so much as trying to grab stuff and push hisself off the car.

Q.   Could it have happened and you missed it?

A.   Him striking the officer?

Q.   Right, some type of physical altercation with the officer inside the car.

A.   Like I said, I was standing so close and directly in the doorway with him the whole time he's pulling away, but Big Mike never swung his left arm at all or never put his left arm inside the window, anything like that. And 'cause the officer had his right arm, I'm almost positive Big Mike couldn't like hit the officer.

Q.   Okay, you said you were sure he never touched the gun?

A.   Yes, ma'am, correct.

Q.   Dorian, do you understand, I don't know, I'm not a physics person or anything, but you know you kind of said to yourself that Mike Brown was in an advantageous position and that he was standing on his feet outside the vehicle.

A.   Correct.

Q.   And the officer is seated inside the vehicle?

A.   Correct.

Q.   Hard to figure out why he couldn't break free; if the officer just has him with his left hand?

A.   Uh-huh.

Q.   First of all by the neck?

A.   Uh-huh.

Q.   And then by his shirt?

A.   Correct.

Q.   So you understand, it might be difficult to grasp why if Big Mike had fallen over, wouldn't just his sheer weight have caused his shirt to rip?

A. Once you have a grasp on something, I don't care if someone's really strong, if you have a good grip on it, you can pretty much hold on to a lot, if someone's stronger than you. Not his flesh so much more, but more his shirt. I'm not letting this shirt go sort of thing.

Q. Just to clarify, you didn't see him get out of the car, but you saw him standing up and fully erect out of the car later, correct?

A. The police officer?

Q. Yeah, right.

A. Yes, I did, correct.

Q. Okay, so the first shot goes off in the car while he has Big Mike's hand?

A. Yes, ma'am.

Q. Right arm?

A. At this time with the gun out, he don't have much of the flesh so much as his shirt.

Q. Okay.

A. A real tight grip on the shirt now.

Q. Does he have on a long- or short-sleeve shirt?

A. Short-sleeve shirt.

Q. So you told us the position of the hand when the gun goes off, the first shot inside the car, he's in the car, while the shot you said went out of the car?

A. Yes, ma'am.

Q. It hit Big Mike and then what?

A. I sees the fire come out of the gun and the shot go off, then I see Big Mike, I see the blood come down his right side, I see the blood come down. He kind of looks at my face and sees my eyes and that was when the officer lets go and we was both able to run. That's when I turn and run. Big Mike was right behind me.

Q. Okay.

A. I don't know if the officer's coming towards Big Mike or just towards both of us, 'cause when I took off running, I was still in front of him.

When I got to the first vehicle, like a Sunfire, a small gray vehicle, the officer was not yet out of his car. I know he was still in his car, 'cause I was able to run to the little car and like stand, but I was standing behind the car.

When Big Mike ran past me, he looked directly at me and said, "Keep running, bro!" And at that time is when I kinda hear a car door opening, so I figure the officer is outta his car now.

As Big Mike run past me and sees me, he keeps goin'. He makes it past the second car and I'm not looking around, but I kinda glance over my right and sees the officer now. He's walking but he's kinda walking fast—not running or nothin' like that, but he has his weapon drawn.

Q. Just like you are doing now? (indicating)

A. Yeah, like this (indicating), his weapon is drawn and he's walking fast. He's not saying nothin' at this time, just concentrating on walking.

And I watch the officer walk past, he just keeps walking past and I'm watching him and I'm in awe. After he walked past me, I kinda stand up more.

I'm watching the officer, he's walking and Big Mike gets past the third car— the final car before the second shot. The officer fires the second shot—pow! I don't know what it hit, 'cause I wasn't that close to Big Mike to see that it hit him, but the way he jerked and just stopped in his tracks, I senses that he was hit again.

Q. What is Big Mike doing?

A. At that time, Big Mike's hands was up, but not so much up in the air, 'cause he had been hit somewhere already. It was like his one hand is up and this hand is kinda like down, sorta.

Q. His hands were nowheres near his waist?

A. No, his hands never went down to his waist—nothin' like that—he didn't even have a belt on.

Q. Was he sagging, were his pants sagging, since you said he wasn't wearing a belt?

A. No, he didn't look like he was sagging.

Q. That's okay if he was—I'm trying to get the picture.

A. At that time I wasn't looking for something like that, I was looking more at him and the officer, 'cause a how he stopped. Big Mike looks to be shot again, so now I'm really fearing like, wow, he looks to be shot twice, but I didn't know for sure.

Q. All right. When Big Mike turns around, show us where his hands were.

A. His hands, this one is higher (indicating), the other one is a little lower, so he was definitely hit with the first shot. I could tell he was injured 'cause of where this hand was. As I'm looking at him, he didn't really say I'm unarmed—he said, "I don't have a gun," but he's still mad en' has his angry face.

And he never starts running 'cause, you know, he's hit. And before he can even get it out that he don't have a gun, that's when several more shots came.

Q. You heard him say that he didn't have a gun?

A. I sees him start to say something.

Q. What did you hear him say, if anything?

A. I heard him start to say, "I don't have ... , but you know, in my state of mind, in my shock ...

Q. Let me just make sure I understand, because this is important. Does he actually say, did you hear him say, "I don't have a gun" or is this what you are thinking he's trying to say?

A. No, he definitely said, "I don't have a gun."

Q. You heard him say that?

A. Yes, he said, "I don't have a gun."

Q. Okay.

A. The second time he started to say it, you know, he couldn't get the full sentence out before the other shots hit his body. And I stood and watched face-to-face as every shot was fired and as his body went down and his body never—his body kinda collapsed and he just fell down.

Q. Was he walking towards the officer as he was collapsing?

A. Like he couldn't get a step off. When he was trying to say again that he didn't have a gun, it was like he was gonna step close to the officer.

Q. And were shots being fired as Big Mike was going down?

A. When the officer fires that last shot, Big Mike was so close to the ground, it looks to me like he was already on the ground.

Q. After he stopped shooting, what did Officer Wilson do next?

A. When he was done shooting, the officer, he just kinda stood there.

Q. Did he check to see if there was a weapon anywhere?

A. No, ma'am.

Q. What do you mean, he just stood there?

A. After firing the final shots—the rippling shots, 'cause there's only one rippling shot—the officer kinda just stood there. And I see Big Mike on the ground, he's not moving, breathing, or nothin' like that. It wasn't like a full two seconds before I took off running, I just …

Q. So you didn't see the officer when he went back to his car, or when he left the scene, or anything like that?

A. No, I didn't see him go back to his car or nothin' when I took off running.

Q. Go ahead and finish.

A. You can see where my apartment is, how close the street is. When I came back to the street, I got to about where I could still see Big Mike was still lying in the street in the same position he was in when he got shot, but I didn't see the officer no more. I saw his cruiser—his car was still there—it didn't look like he was inside the car.

I continued to walk along, 'cause now there's a lot of people outside, but I didn't see the officer no more, I didn't see no officers on the scene.

Q. That is what my question was, so your answer is that there were no police officers on the scene at this time when you walk back?

A. No, ma'am.

Q. People from the neighborhood?

A. Yes.

Q. How long were you in the house?

A. Not even two or three minutes.

Q. So the road was open between Michael Brown and the police cruiser, with nobody else on the road?

A. Correct.

Q. What did you do when you see him lying there, but no police are around—what do you do?

A. At that time I kinda stood back in the crowd of people starting to come out, 'cause at the time now, a police officer was coming. It wasn't Darren Wilson who came back, but some other officer. He started putting up yellow tape around the area. At that time, he was by hisself.

Q. The next day, did anyone tell you that the police came to (redacted) looking to get a statement?

A. When I come out the next day , the 10th, most people thought I was dead, 'cause they said that they found a body behind Domino's. The media, it was out of control.

Q. You said several times that the police officer didn't say stop or freeze or halt. But he did say I'll shoot, I'll shoot … ?

A. When a police officer says I'll shoot, that doesn't mean stop or halt. That means either get out of the way or protect yourself. If he really wanted someone to stop, they have lots of phrases that they teach the first day at police academy like halt or freeze.

Q. And then, as Mike Brown ran away, Officer Wilson stepped towards Mike Brown and fired one shot?

A. Yes, ma'am.

Q. And you believe that shot hit Big Mike?

A. Yes, ma'am.

Q. While Big Mike is running away?

A. Yes. His back is facing me and the officer, 'cause Big Mike is ahead of us now. So he's the farthest one, the officer is behind him, and I'm behind the officer, but basically Big Mike's back is facing both of us.

Q. Now, Mike is running, at this point, right?

A. Yes, ma'am.

Q. Can you just stand up for me and show me what position Mike's body was in when you believe the officer shot him?

A. The second time?

Q. Yes, can you show me how it looked to you from behind as Big Mike was running away?

A. He's running with his arms down. Once the second shot fires, I sees his body do like a jerking movement, not to where it looked like he got hit in his back, but I knew it maybe could have grazed him.

Q. Okay, when you saw this happen, at that point, his arms are not up, raised up, correct?

A. He stops and he turns around.

Q. Okay, and then Big Mike doesn't proceed toward the officer?

A. No, ma'am.

Q. And as we explained to you before this started, we're trying to get to the truth?

A. Yes, ma'am.

Q. And this next question is so important, because we don't want any people saying, "Well, yeah, I talked to somebody who told me about this." Do you know if there is someone out there who might have seen any part of this?

A. I'm real surprised you have so many witnesses to this, 'cause before it happened, I only saw one person. I didn't see nobody at first, and I only saw her, 'cause before the first shot when the police stopped us, she was on her balcony.

Q. Is there anything you want to tell us that we just didn't think to ask that you think is important, any other information about this case?

A. Yes, in spite of everybody's opinion of me, my dirty past and criminal record, that day I felt like even though the store thing had happened, it didn't feel right for someone to lose their life.

Q. You mentioned something, you know, the grand jurors may want to factor in to their discussion. You said something about a criminal record?

A. Yes, I see they dug through years past to find an incident in Jefferson City, but what they keep leaving out is I was a freshman in college—everybody makes, you know, crazy little moves their freshman year. I was just beginning, I was getting out, I was breaking out of my kid years. Basically, all I keep seeing is slander on my name.

Q. We don't want to slander you, but we just want all the information you can give us. What is the nature of this 'thing' in Jefferson City—what happened?

A.   Basically, me walking with a group. So we was walking through some apartments, one of the guys grabs a package and rips it open. So I guess whoever's package it was, they made the call saying somebody stole something. And when the police came, they run the camera back.

Q.   Did you get charged with that?

A.   Nope, I didn't get charged with it, but I had to go to court on two other charges.

Q.   What were those charges?

A.   I had a false report to an officer, a stealing charge. I was fed up with being stopped by off-campus and on-campus police, 'cause of the way they look at people from St. Louis. I just said, you know what, Jefferson City school, Lincoln University, was not for me at the time, so I left.

Q.   I just want to clarify what you had mentioned—the stealing thing and then you said you had a false police report?

A.   Those police was like saying, "You're not gonna give me nothin', so I'm just going to write down that you gave me a false report." But I really didn't do nothin'.

Ms Whirley: Anything else? Dorian, we appreciate you coming.

END OF EXAMINATION

State of Missouri v. Darren Wilson

Grand Jury Volume V

September 16, 2014

Excerpts from Grand Jury Volume V.

The testimony of Ferguson Police Officer Darren Wilson:

FOR THE STATE: MS SHELIA WHIRLEY

                         MS KATHI ALIZADEH

BACK FROM RECESS

MS. ALIZADEH:

This is Kathi Alizadeh. It is about 3:20 on the 16th of September. We are about to call our final witness, Darren Wilson. And, as usual, Shelia and I will be asking him questions and you are free to ask questions, either interrupting or wait until the end, however you feel is better for the flow of things.

Officer Wilson is here and prepared to answer questions. You heard him talk and we have heard testimony that he has had an attorney during parts of this. Therefore, I would tell you that any conversations he has had with his attorney are what we call privileged communication, so you cannot ask him questions like, what did you tell your attorney or what did your attorney say about that—is that clear?

Any other questions that you think are relevant are fair game, but any client/attorney communication are privileged and you cannot inquire about that. All right, that being said, I am going to let Officer Wilson walk in and be sworn.

EXAMINATION BY MS WHIRLEY:

Q.   So to introduce yourself to the grand jurors, tell us your name and spell it for the court reporter, please.

A.   My name is Darren Wilson. D-A-R-R-E-N, last name W-I-L-S-O-N.

Q.   Have you appeared before this grand jury before?

A.   No, I have not.

Q.   So nobody is familiar to you here, correct?

A.   No, ma'am.

Q.   All right. Are you currently on leave or what's your status right now?

A.   I am on Paid Administrative Leave.

Q. Now, we have never met before, have we?

A. No, ma'am.

Q. However, did we meet right before you came here today, when I talked to you and your attorneys?

A. Correct.

Q. And you came here voluntarily?

A. Correct.

Q. And you were told that if you wanted to consult with your attorneys, you could?

A. Correct.

Q. Okay. And you want to be here and tell the jurors what happened—is that correct?

A. That's correct.

Q. So August 9, 2014, you worked as a police officer for the Ferguson police department?

A. Correct.

Q. That means you are a certified police officer?

A. Correct.

Q. Had you completed all your training and kept up with your continuing education as a certified officer does?

A. Yes, ma'am.

Q. You have the power of arrest?

A. Correct.

Q. In the state of Missouri?

A. Yes, ma'am.

Q. What's your height?

A. 6'4", just a shy under 6'4".

Q. A little under 6'4"?

A. Yes, ma'am.

Q. And how much do you currently weigh?

A.   210-ish.

Q.   That's been your weight for a while?

A.   Yeah, it fluctuates between 205, 212, 213, something like that.

Q.   Of course, everybody knows why we're here, so let's just get to it.

A.   Okay.

Q.   Let's talk about your day on August the 9th. What shift did you work?

A.   Day shift.

Q.   And what shift would that be, what hours?

A.   6:30 a.m. to 6:30 p.m.

Q.   Twelve-hour shift?

A.   Correct.

Q.   Had you worked the day before?

A.   Yes, I had.

Q.   Same shift?

A.   Yes.

Q.   You weren't working like midnights the night before?

A.   No, ma'am.

Q.   When you started your shift, did anything happen that you consider very eventful? I mean, earlier that day, prior to 10:00 let's say, 10:00 a.m.

A.   No, ma'am.

Q.   Had you answered any calls prior to 10:00 a.m.?

A.   I don't recall, I don't believe so, but I don't recall—nothing stands out in my memory.

Q.   It was a pretty quiet day initially?

A.   Yes, ma'am.

Q.   Now, at some point you had a sick call—a sick baby, I think?

A.   Yes, ma'am.

Q.   And that would have been 11-ish or so?

A.   I think it was around 11:30-ish, somewhere in that vicinity.

Q. That was near the Canfield Green Apartments?

A. Yes, ma'am, it was actually past them in the adjoining apartment complex.

Q. And what do they call those apartments?

A. I believe that apartment is called North Winds.

Q. North Winds. Okay. And it is like east of the Canfield Green, behind those apartments?

A. Correct.

Q. When you went on that call, did you have assistance?

A. No, I did not.

Q. All right.

A. Not police assistance.

Q. No police assistance?

A. No.

Q. You handled that call by yourself?

A. Yes, ma'am.

Q. And did you have any confrontation with anybody or was it pretty much a matter-of-fact call?

A. It was a pretty laid-back call. It was for a sick infant, I believe, only a couple months old.

Q. Okay.

A. I believe she had a fever, I'm not 100 percent sure.

Q. Let me ask this question, can everybody hear him? Speak up. I usually stand in the back of the room so we can have a conversation. As you can tell, my voice really carries, so try to speak up so everybody can hear you.

A. Okay.

Q. So the baby was an infant?

A. Correct.

Q. Was the baby not breathing? What was the call, do you recall?

A. I believe it was for a fever.

Q.   Fever you said? Ambulance arrived?

A.   Arrived.

Q.   Mother?

A.   Yes, ambulance arrived at the same time I …

Q.   Okay. Baby was transported to the hospital with the mother. After that, what did you do?

A.   I returned to my vehicle and then started to leave the apartment complex.

Q.   Okay. Did you get any other calls between the time of the sick baby call and your interaction with Michael Brown and Dorian Johnson?

A.   While on the sick case call, a call came out for a stealing in progress from the local market on West Florissant and the suspects were traveling towards QT. I didn't hear the entire call, I was on my portable radio, which isn't exactly the best. I did hear that a suspect was wearing a black shirt and that a box of cigarillos was stolen.

Q.   Okay. And was this your call or you just heard the call? That call?

A.   It was not my call—I heard the call. Some other officers were dispatched too.

Q.   Was it that call that you were going to go to also?

A.   No.

Q.   So you weren't really geared to handle that call?

A.   No.

0.   Tell us how you were dressed that day on August the 9th?

A.   How I was dressed?

Q.   Yes.

A.   I was wearing my full department uniform, light duty boots, dark navy blue pants, my issue duty belt, with my uniform shirt, and that was it.

Q.   All right. And so when you say, when you are in uniform, you were not a detective?

A.   No, ma'am.

Q.   You weren't dressed the way you are dressed here today?

A. No, ma'am.

Q. So your uniform is like a uniform police officer and when you are walking around I can clearly see, oh, that's a police officer?

A. Yes, ma'am, I believe it is French blue uniform shirt, has patches for Ferguson on both sides, badge, and name tag.

Q. Okay. And you were in what type of vehicle?

A. I was in a Chevy Tahoe police vehicle fully marked with a light bar.

Q. Fully marked, okay. Tell us, you were mentioning your radio or what is this you spoke about?

A. Walkie is what we normally call it.

Q. Like a walkie-talkie or something? On your belt?

A. Yes, ma'am.

Q. And it did work that day?

A. Yes

Q. Okay. And it was on which shoulder?

A. I wear it on my left shoulder.

Q. Are you left- or right-handed?

A. I'm right-handed.

Q. Okay. Tell us what else is on your duty belt.

A. I'll go in order: magazine pouches sit right here, my weapon is on my right hip, I have an ASP that sits kind of behind to the right of me, and then a set of handcuffs, another set of handcuffs, my OC spray or mace is on this side, and then my radio and that's it.

Q. Okay. So your mace is on your left side and your gun is on your right side?

A. Correct.

Q. What type of weapon did you carry?

A. I carry SIG Sauer, a P229 .40 caliber.

Q. How many cartridges or bullets would it hold?

A. It has 12 in the magazine and one goes into the chamber, so a total of 13.

Q. You had a couple spare magazines on your belt?

A. Correct.

Q. That had 12 each?

A. Correct.

Q. Did you carry a taser?

A. No.

Q. Why not?

A. I normally don't carry a taser. We only have a select amount of space on our belt. Usually there is one available, but I usually elect not to carry one. It is not the most comfortable thing. They are very large, and I don't have a lot of room in the front for it to be positioned.

Q. Had you been trained on how to use a taser?

A. Yes, ma'am.

Q. Have you ever used a taser before?

A. I believe I have, but it wasn't one that I carried. It was one that I used from someone else on a scene. I can't remember that time or where I used it.

Q. You prefer not to have a taser?

A. Correct.

Q. So that day you had mace, you said, on your left side?

A. Correct.

Q. All right. You are coming west, is it on Canfield Drive?

A. Yes, I started out on Glenark and then I turned onto Bahama and then onto Glen Owen, and then I turned on Windward, which actually turns into Canfield Green and that's where I was going west on that.

Q. West on Canfield Drive?

A. Yes, ma'am.

Q. Okay. We are going to get a map here shortly so you can kind of map it out for us.

So as you are going west on Canfield Drive, what happens?

A.   As I was going west on Canfield, I observed two men in the middle of the street, walking along the double yellow line, single file order.

Q.   Okay. And you say something to them—did they say something to you first?

A.   No, you want me to go with the whole thing?

Q.   Sure, go ahead, let's start there.

A.   I see them walking down the middle of the street. And the first thing that struck me was they're walking in the middle of the street. I had already seen a couple cars trying to pass, but they couldn't have normal traffic, because these two guys were in the middle, so one had to stop to let the car go around and then another car would come. And the next thing I noticed was the size of the individuals, because either the first one was really small or the second one was really big.

And just for the conversation, I didn't know this then, but the first one's name was Dorian Johnson, the second one was Michael Brown. I discovered that the following day when I learned their names. I had never seen them before.

And then the next thing I noticed was that Brown had bright yellow socks on that had green marijuana leaves as a pattern on them. They were the taller socks that go halfway up the shin.

As I approached them, I stopped a couple feet in front of Johnson, so as they were walking towards me, I am going towards them. And I allowed him to keep walking towards my window, which was down. As Johnson came around my driver's side mirror I said, "Why don't you guys walk on the sidewalk?" He kept walking, and as he is walking he said, "We are almost at our destination."

Q.   Do you think he used those words destination, "We are almost to our destination"?

A.   Yes, ma'am. He said, "We are almost to our destination," and he pointed in the direction over my vehicle—like in a northeasterly direction. And as he did that, he kept walking. Brown was starting to come around the mirror and as he came around the mirror I said, "Well, what's wrong with the sidewalk?" Brown then replied, um—it has vulgar language.

Q.   You can say it.

A.   Brown then replied, "Fuck what you have to say." And when he said that, it drew my attention totally to Brown. It was very unusual and not expected from a simple request.

When I start looking at Brown, the first thing I notice is in his right hand—his hand is full of cigarillos, so I look in my mirror and did a double-check. Johnson was wearing a black shirt, so these are the two from the stealing.

They kept walking—never once stopped, never got on the sidewalk—they just stayed in the middle of the road.

I radioed, "Frank 21," which is my call sign that day, "I'm on Canfield with two, send me another car."

I then placed my car in reverse and backed up just past them and angled the back of my vehicle to kind of cut them off and keep them somewhat contained.

As I did that, I go to open my door and I say, "Hey, come here for a minute," to Brown. As I'm opening the door he turns, faces me, looks at me and says, "What the fuck are you going to do about it?" and shuts my door, slammed it shut. I haven't even got it open enough to get my leg out, it was only open a few inches.

I looked at him and told him to get back, but he was just staring at me, almost like trying to intimidate or overpower me. The intense face he had was just not what I expected from any of this.

I then opened my door again and used it to push him backwards, and while I'm doing that I tell him to "Get the fuck back," and then I use my door to push him some more.

Q.   You tell him to, "Get the fuck back"?

A.   Yes.

Q.   Okay.

A.   He then grabs my door again and slams it shut. That time is when I saw him coming into my vehicle. His head was higher than the top of my vehicle, so I see him ducking and as he is ducking, his hands are up and he is coming in my vehicle.

I shielded myself in this type of manner (officer demonstrates) and kind of looked away, so I don't remember seeing him come at me, but I was hit right here in the side of the face with a fist. I don't think it was

69

a full-on swing, but not a full shot. I think my arm deflected some of it, but he still made a significant amount of contact with my face.

Q. Now, he was hitting you with what hand?

A. I believe it was the right hand, just judging by how we were situated.

Q. Right?

A. But like I said, I had turned away and was shielding my eyes.

Q. Where did you see the cigarillos?

A. They were in his right hand.

Q. Okay, were any broken cigarillos or anything else in your car later?

A. No, I don't remember seeing anything on the ground or anywhere else.

Q. Okay.

A. After he hit me then, it stopped for a second. I remember getting hit and he grabbed me and pulled, and then it stopped. When I looked up, if this is my car door, I'm sitting here facing that way, and he's here. He turns like this and now I see the cigarillos in his left hand. He's going like this and he says, "Hey man, hold these."

Q. So it starts out with the cigarillos in his right hand?

A. Correct.

Q. And at this point, they are in his left hand?

A. Correct.

Q. He didn't have like two hands of cigarillos?

A. No, I only saw them in one hand.

Q. You only saw them in one, okay, go ahead.

A. And he reaches back and he says, "Hey, man, hold these." I'm assuming he means Johnson, but I couldn't see from my line of sight.

Q. But you could tell he was giving Johnson the cigarillos?

A. Yes, I saw them in his hand.

Q. All right.

A. And he said, "Hey, man, hold these." And at that point, I tried to hold his right arm because it was like this in my car. This is my car window. I tried to hold his right arm and use my left hand to get out so I could have some type of control and not be trapped in my car any more. When I grabbed him, the only way I can describe it is I felt like a five-year-old holding onto Hulk Hogan.

Q. Holding on to what?

A. Hulk Hogan, that's just how big he felt and how small I felt just from grasping his arm.

As I'm trying to open the door, I can't really get it open, because he is standing only maybe six inches from my door. As I was trying to pull the handle, I see his hand coming back around like this and he hit me with this part of his right hand here, just a full swing all the way back around and hit me right here. (indicating)

After he did that, I remember thinking, How do I get this guy away from me? What can I do to not get beaten up inside my car?

I remember having my hands up and I thought to myself, You know, what do I do now?

I considered using my mace. However, I wasn't willing to sacrifice my left hand, which is blocking my face, to go for it. I couldn't reach around on my right to get it and if I would have gotten it out, the chances of it being effective were slim to none. His hands were in front of his face, so it would have blocked the mace from hitting him in the face. If any of that had gotten on me, I would have been out of the game, since I know what it does to me. I wear contacts, so if that touches any part of my eyes, I can't see at all.

Like I said, I don't carry a taser, so I considered my ASP, but to get that out since I kind of was sitting on it, I usually have to lean forward and pull myself forward to the steering wheel to get it out. Again, I wasn't willing to let go of the one defense I had against being hit. The whole time, I can't tell you if he was swinging at me or grabbing or pushing me or what, but there was just lots of stuff going on and I was looking down trying to figre out what to do.

Also, when I was grabbing my ASP, I knew if I did even get it out, I'm not going to be able to expand it inside the car. I wasn't sure if I was going to be able to make a swing that will be effective in any manner.

Next, I considered my flashlight. I keep that on the passenger side of the car. I wasn't going to reach over like this to grab it and even if I did, wasn't sure if it would even be effective. We are so close and confined.

So the only other option I thought I had was my gun. I drew it and turned. It's kind of hard to describe it, I turn and I go like this. He is standing here. I said, "Get back or I'm going to shoot you."

He immediately grabs my gun and says, "You are too much of a pussy to shoot me." Do you have a picture of the way he grabbed it?

Q. I do have some pictures of your gun. Well, you can tell us if it is your gun, but I believe it is.

A. My gun was basically pointed this way. I'm in my car and he's here. It's pointed this way, but he grabs it with his right hand—not his left. He twists it and then he digs it down into my hip. (indicating)

Q. So during this time, you said Michael Brown is striking you in the face through the car door.

A. Right.

Q. And it was your opinion that you needed to pull out your weapon. Why did you feel that way? I don't want to put words in your mouth.

A. I felt that another one of those punches in my face could knock me out or worse. I mean, he's obviously bigger than I was and stronger and I've already taken two to the face, so the third one could be fatal if he hit me right.

Q. You thought he could hit you and it would be a fatal injury?

A. Or at least I'd be unconscious and then who knows what would happen to me after that.

Q. You had not ever met Michael Brown or Dorian Johnson before this date?

A. No, ma'am.

Q. Okay. Anything else? Tell us about your injuries.

A. I had a swollen right cheek, and they said my left was swollen too. I had scratches around my hairline and on my back and I think on the side of my neck, but that's all I remember.

Q. Any injuries to your hand?

A. No.

Q. All right. So you suffered the injury to your face, and you showed us where the gun was grabbed. Take us from the time when you struggled for the gun.

A. He grabs my gun and says, "You are too much of a pussy to shoot me." The gun goes down into my hip and at that point, I thought I was getting shot. I can feel his fingers try to get inside the trigger guard with my finger and I distinctly remember envisioning a bullet going into my leg. I thought that was the next step.

Q. I'm going to stand back so you can talk louder.

A. As I'm looking at the gun, I'm not paying attention to Brown. All I can focus on is just this gun in my leg.

I was able to kind of shift slightly like this and then push the gun down, because he is pushing down to keep it pinned on my leg. When I slid, I let him use his momentum to push it down, so it was kind of pointed to where the seat buckle would attach to the floorboard on the side of my car.

Next thing I remember is putting my left hand on the gun like this, putting my elbow into the back of my seat, and just pushing forward with all I could.

Q. Were you saying anything?

A. I don't know.

Q. You don't know if he was saying anything either?

A. I heard stuff, but I couldn't tell you what it was.

Q. Okay.

A. Like I said, I was just so focused on getting the gun out of me. When I did get it up, he is still holding onto it, so when I pull the trigger, nothing happens—it just clicks. I pull it again, but it just clicks again.

At this point, I'm wondering why this isn't working—this guy is going to kill me if he gets ahold of my gun. I pull it a third time and it goes off, shooting through my door panel. I think that kind of startles him and me at the same time.

When I see the glass come up, a chunk about that big comes across my right hand and then I notice I have blood on the back of my hand.

After seeing the blood on my hand, I look at him and he was, like this is my car door, he was here and he kind of steps back and went like this. (indicating)

And then, after he does that, he looks up at me and has the most intense aggressive face. The only way I can describe it is it looks like a demon—that's how angry he looks. He comes back towards me again with his hands up.

At that point, I just go like this and try to pull the trigger again, but click, nothing happens.

Q.   When you say he came back to you with his hands up, describe to us what he is doing.

A.   Last thing I saw was this coming at me.

Q.   Was it a fist?

A.   I just saw his hands up. I don't know if they are closed yet or on the way to being closed, but I saw that face coming at me again, and I just go like this and shield my face.

Q.   And you did what?

A.   Went like this and shielded my face.

Q.   Did he hit you at that time?

A.   Yes.

Q.   Okay. Go ahead.

A.   So I pull the trigger, but it just clicks that time. Without even looking, I grab the top of my gun—the slide—and I rack it. Still not looking, but just holding my hand up, I pull the trigger again and it goes off. When I look back after that—

Q.   So how many times does it go off in the car?

A.   It went off twice in the car. Pull, click, click, went off, click, went off, so twice in the car.

Q.   Are you certain?

A.   Yes.

Q.   Okay.

A.   When I look up after that, I see him start to run and I see a cloud of dust behind him. I get out of my car and as I'm getting out, I tell dispatch, "Shots fired, send me more cars."

We start running, kind of the same direction that Johnson had pointed—across the street like a diagonal, kind of like where the parking lot came in for Copper Creek Court and Canfield, right at that intersection. I remember him running towards the light pole there.

We pass two cars that are behind my police car while we are running. I think the second one is a Pontiac Grand Am, a green one. I don't know if it is a two-door or a four-door, I just remember seeing a Pontiac green Grand Am.

When I pass the second one, about that same time, he stops running and he is at that light pole. When he stops, I stop and then he starts to turn around. I tell him to get on the ground, get on the ground.

He turns, and when he looks at me, he makes a like grunting, like an aggravated sound and he starts coming back towards me. His first step is kind of like a stutter step to start running. When he does that, his left hand goes into a fist and he goes to his side. His right hand goes under his shirt in his waistband and he starts running at me.

Q. You say under his shirt?

A. Yes.

Q. Was he wearing a shirt that was longer than his waistband?

A. Yes, ma'am.

Q. So he goes up under his shirt?

A. Yes.

Q. Okay. Go ahead.

A. That was all done, like I said, in the first step, his first stride coming back towards me.

As he is coming towards me, I keep telling him to get on the ground, but he doesn't. I shoot a series of shots. I don't know how many, I just know I shoot my gun.

I know I miss a couple, I don't know how many, but I know I hit him at least once, because I see his body kind of jerk or flinch.

I remember having tunnel vision on his right hand, because I'm just focusing on that hand as I am shooting.

Well, after the last shot, my tunnel vision kind of opens up. I remember seeing the smoke from the gun and I look at him, but he's still coming at me and hasn't slowed down.

I start backpedaling and again, I tell him get on the ground, get on the ground, but he doesn't. I shoot another round of shots. Again, I don't recall how many it was or if I hit him every time, but I know I hit him at least once, because he flinches again.

At that point, it looks like he is almost bulking up to run through the shots, like it was making him mad that I'm shooting at him.
And his face is looking straight through me, like I am not even there, I wasn't even anything in his way.

Well, he keeps coming at me after that again, during the pause I tell him to get on the ground, get on the ground. However, he still keeps coming at me and gets about 8 to 10 feet away. At this point, I'm backing up pretty rapidly. I'm backpedaling pretty good, because I know if he reaches me, he'll kill me.

He starts to lean forward as he got that close, like he was going to just tackle me, just go right through me.

Q.   Can you demonstrate for us how he was leaning forward?

A.   His one hand was in a fist at his side and his other was in his waistband under his shirt, and he was like this—just coming straight at me like he was going to run right through me. And when he gets about 8 to 10 feet away, I look down, I remember looking at my sights and firing. Since all I see is his head, that's what I shoot.

I don't know how many times he is hit, but I know at least once, because I see the last one go into him. When that happens, the demeanor of his face goes blank and the aggression is gone. I know he stopped and that the threat was stopped.

When he falls, he falls on his face. I remember his feet coming up, like he had so much momentum carrying him forward that when he fell, his feet kind of came up a little bit and then they rested.

At that point, I got back on the radio and said, "Send me a supervisor and every car you've got."

Q.   Okay, so when the shots were first fired in your car, you said you believe you fired two shots in the car?

A. Yes, two actually went off in the car.

Q. Two went off in the car. And at this point, the second shot, is that when he ran?

A. After the second shot, yes.

Q. After the second shot. Are you still in the car?

A. When he starts to run?

Q. Yes.

A. Yes, ma'am.

Q. Okay. At this time, do you say, "Shots fired"?

A. As I'm exiting the car to chase him, yes.

Q. Did you know that your radio dispatch did not go out?

A. No, I didn't find out until later. While I was actually driving back to the station, I realize that my portable radio is on channel 3, but our main channel is channel 1.

Q. So to your knowledge, nobody heard you say, "Shots fired"?

A. To my knowledge.

Q. Okay.

A. They did ask me why my radio for the car was laying on the floor-board and asked if I used that. I don't remember using that radio. I, for some reason, remember using this one. It could have been sitting in my lap, but there was also that chance that I used the other one. I don't know which one I used.

Q. All right. So you're in the car, you fire two shots and he's running. then you get out of the car to chase after him. Tell us your ratio-nale—what you are thinking now?

A. When I'm chasing him?

Q. Yes. You get out of the car and run after him.

A. My main goal is to keep on him and just keep him contained until my people arrived. I know I had called for backup and they were already in the area for the stealing that was originally reported. I thought if I can buy 30 seconds of time, that is my original goal when I try to get him to come to the car. If I could do that, someone else will be here, so we can make the arrest. That way, nothing happens and we are all good, but it didn't happen that way.

So when he ran, I was thinking, just stay with him, because someone is going to be here and we'll get him.

Q. When the second shot is fired inside the car, did you think he was hit at all?

A. No, I thought I missed.

Q. Both shots? You didn't see any blood on him?

A. Judging by his reaction and the way he went back, I thought the first shot went through the door and hit him in the leg or the hip—that's what I thought.

Q. Okay.

A. When I shot the second one, I saw a cloud of dust and him running, so I knew I missed.

Q. Okay. So you got out of the car, you are running, and you are telling him to stop—is that right?

A. Correct.

Q. And he's not listening?

A. No, not until he gets to the light pole and that's when he stops.

Q. So what now?

A. He gets to that light pole at that intersection.

Q. Are you firing at him while he's running?

A. No, ma'am.

Q. Is Dorian Johnson anywhere around?

A. I never saw him after the very beginning. Once he walked past my car, I never saw him again. [Author's comment: the little shit took off like a scalded duck!]

Q. Okay. All right. At some point, you say Michael Brown does turn around?

A. Yes, ma'am.

Q. Any idea what happened to make him turn around or did he just all of a sudden turn around?

A. No, he just turns around. His reaction to the whole thing was something I've never seen before—so much aggression happening so quickly from a simple request to just walk on the sidewalk.

Q. Okay. Because you never did talk to him about the cigarillos or the stealing at the Ferguson Market?

A. No, I never had the chance to.

Q. All right. You said when he's coming back at you with his right hand in his waistband and kind of charging, that's when you fired the last shots?

A. Yes, ma'am.

Q. And he went down?

A. Yes, ma'am.

Q. Did you think he was dead at this point?

A. Yes, I did.

Q. What did you do after that when he goes down?

A. After that is when I get back on the radio and I say, "Send me a supervisor and every car you have."

Seconds later is when officer [redacted] followed by officer [redacted] arrive. I believe they were the ones that were assigned to the stealing call originally. [redacted] They walked up and said, "Darren, what do you need?"

Q. Ms. Alizadeh: Said what?

A. Darren, what do you need? I don't remember what my reply was, but he asked, "Did you call for an ambulance?" I said I haven't, so will you? I remember him calling twice, like he was about from me to you away on the radio calling.

Then I look across and [redacted] was starting to tape off the area, but I notice that all of our cars are parked this way. Brown is lying here and nothing is on this side. I told [redacted] to move his car to this side to block that side of the street off. After he does that, he resumes taping.

I walk to my car, put my gun up, and I start to walk away from the scene. Suddenly, I walk back to my car, thinking that I don't know if the door was open or shut, but I think it was shut, so I open the door. At that time, my sergeant pulls up and I walk over to him.

Q. Ms. Whirley: This is Sergeant [redacted]?

A. Yes, ma'am.

Q. Okay.

A. I don't remember what started the conversation. He says something first, but I say, "I have to tell you what happened." So he goes, "What happened?"

I say, "I had to kill him." He goes, "You what?"

Then he says, "Take my car and leave." So I get into the car and drive to the police station.

Q. In your mind, Michael Brown grabbing the gun is what makes a difference and where you feel you had to use a weapon to stop him?

A. Yes. Brown hitting me in the face was enough, in my mind, to authorize the use of force.

Q. Okay. So if he would not have grabbed your gun while he was hitting you in the face, everything was the same, but he would not have grabbed the gun, you still would have used deadly force?

A. My gun was already being presented as a deadly force option while he was hitting me in the face.

Q. Okay, all right. So then you go to the station?

A. Yes.

Q. And what happens, you go alone?

A. Yes.

Q. Before you leave for the station, a crowd is developing, right?

A. Correct.

Q. Do you hear what the crowd is saying? I know you are in a pretty stressful situation, but do you understand or hear anything that they're saying?

A. I hear yelling and screaming, and as I'm walking back to my car, a white ford truck pulls up. I remember someone saying, "Is that so and so?" A female driver gets out. [redacted] said, "Ma'am, we don't know." I hear her say, "I think it is so and so," and then she screams and that's all I hear.

Q. Okay. We're going to go with you to the station in just a minute, but

I wanted to ask you about your relationship with the residents in the Canfield Green Apartments.

A. Uh-huh.

Q. Did you guys have a volatile, well, how can I put this—did you really get along well with the folks that lived in that apartment—not you personally, but I mean the police in general?

A. It's an anti-police area, for sure.

Q. And when you say anti-police, tell me more.

A. Many gangs reside in or associate with that area. A lot of violence occurs there, with countless gun and drug activity, so it is just not a very well-liked community. That community doesn't like the police.

Q. Were you pretty much on high alert being in that community by yourself, especially when Michael Brown said, "Fuck what you say," which is what I think he said?

A. Yes.

Q. You were on pretty high alert at that point, knowing the vicinity and the area that you're in?

A. Yes, that's not an area where you can take anything lightly. Like I said, it is a hostile environment. Some good people are over there, there really are, but I mean there is a huge influx of gang activity in that area.

Q. All right. So when you're driving back to Ferguson, what are you thinking on that drive?

A. I think I'm just kind of in shock with what just happened. I really didn't believe it, because like I said, the whole thing started over a simple question, "Will you just walk on the sidewalk?" It blew up into that riotous scene in just 45 seconds.

And that's the only thing I remember talking about—I hear the car radio going off and mine wasn't. That doesn't make sense.

I did that and still, this one's going off and mine's not. So then I looked at it and saw I was on channel 3. I was like, I don't know what was heard or what wasn't heard.

Q. And that's when you realized that you probably, nobody probably even heard your call for help?

A. Right. I know they heard the initial one, because before I put the Tahoe in reverse, I used the car radio, the car mic, which always is on the Ferguson channel. It never changed, if they even heard anything.

Q. When you first went out on your call to Canfield Green, you said, "I'm going out, Frank 21"?

A. Frank 21.

Q. I'm going out with two, send me a car?

A. I said, "Frank 21, I'm on Canfield with two, send me another car."

Q. It wasn't a stressful situation at that point?

A. No, it wasn't, but I just had that gut feeling that someone else needed to be there and knowing that this guy just stole from the market, because I saw the cigarillos and he had the black shirt. I felt that to affect the arrest, it would be better to have two.

Q. You asked for this other car before any words were exchanged, correct?

A. No, he had already told me, "Fuck what you have to say."

Q. Before you asked for the car, when you said, "I'm Frank 21, I'm at Canfield Green, send me a car," he had already said, "Fuck what you have to say"?

A. Yeah, he had already walked past by my car and said that.

Q. Okay.

A. That's when I see the cigarillos, when he says that and keeps walking. Then I get on the radio and said, "Send me another car."

Q. Okay. All right. So you drive back to Ferguson by yourself, you are at Ferguson, what do you do?

A. I immediately go to the bathroom. On the way back, I find that I had blood on the inside of my left hand and I already know I have it on the back of my right hand. And just from everything we have been taught about blood, you don't want it on you, you don't touch it, you don't come in contact with it.

My original thought was that it was that the glass had cut my hand and wrist, which is why this hand is bleeding. So thinking that I was cut with someone else's blood on me, I had to wash my hands.

I go directly to the bathroom and wash, but when I look again, I still had it like in my cuticles and stuff. I wash my hands again and afterwards, I go to our roll call room.

Q. Let me ask you this, was there a lot of blood?

A. From like my fingertips to about here was blood. (indicating)

Q. Like dripping blood?

A. No, just on the back of my hand. It wasn't like wrapped around, like I dipped my hand in blood, but there was blood on the back of my hand.

Q. One of the grand jurors asked earlier, so you may know the answer to the question—was there blood in Sergeant [redacted] car after you got out of it?

A. I don't know, but I did call him and tell him that I didn't know who is going to drive your car later, but I had blood on my hands. You might want to tell them to wipe down the steering wheel or just be cautious of it, because I never went back and looked at the car.

Q. I see. Okay, so go ahead, after you wash your hands?

A. I then go down the hallway to the roll call room. Once in there, officer [redacted] is in there working on the computer.

Q. And that's a friend of yours?

A. Yeah.

Q. Okay, go ahead.

A. I come in, he looks at me, and I say, "I just had to shoot somebody."

He was kind of in shock and had the computer working on. The guy next to him had the CADament screen that shows the status of all the cars and where they're located. Well, on that one, it is showing all the cars out on Canfield.

He goes, "I was really hoping you weren't involved in that, you know, because any time every car is involved in that, you really don't know what is going to happen, who is going to get hurt."

Q. Okay.

A. I go in there and ask for a pair of gloves.

He comes back and gives me the gloves, so I put them on. I grab an evidence envelope, take my gun out of the holster, and make it safe. I lock the slide back, take the magazine out, and take out the one round that's left in it. I put it all in that bag, seal it with the evidence tape, and then sign it.

Q. And you handle your gun at that time with gloves on?

A. Correct.

Q. And why did you do that?

A. To preserve any evidence on there, as I knew Michael Brown's DNA was on the gun.

Q. How did you know his DNA was on the gun?

A. When I first took it out, without even looking at it, I knew that he had fingerprints and possibly even sweat on it, since it was warmer that day so. When I took it out, I also saw blood on it.

Q. You saw blood?

A. Yes.

Q. And that could have been from when you shot him?

A. Yes.

Q. Okay. Is it procedure for you to make your gun safe in a shooting like this or should someone else do that?

A. I don't really know.

Q. Because that never happened before?

A. Correct.

Q. And you never investigated this type of crime?

A. No, I have not.

Q. Okay, all right. So you knew how to make the gun safe and put it in an evidence envelope based on your training and experience?

A. Yes, I was just trying to preserve all the evidence I could on the weapon. And I knew if I put it into an evidence envelope and sealed it, that it would have no other contact with anybody and it could be as preserved as you could get.

Q. And then what?

A. I sit down and call for an attorney, who represents the police union.

He says he is on his way.

Officer [redacted] says, "Would you like to tell me what happened so I can tell the media?" I said, "No, I don't want to talk right now."

Lieutenant [redacted] came in and asks, "Has anybody told you what's happening?" I said, "I don't know anything that's going on. I leave the scene pretty much right after it happens."

He said, "St. Louis County is investigating." I said, "Okay," and then he leaves. After that, Ferguson Fire Department and EMS from Christian Northeast Hospital show up.

They ask me what happened and I said that I was hit in the face multiple times.

About 20 minutes later, my attorney shows up and we talk for 10 or 15 minutes. My assistant chief shows up and makes the determination that we should go to the hospital, since he notices the swelling on my face.

Detective [redacted] from St. Louis County arrives, informs us he would be investigating the case, and kind of gives us the rundown of what to expect. Then he agrees with going to the hospital. My assistant chief drives me to the hospital with the detective following.

Q. And then what happens after that?

A. At the hospital, we do the interview. When I go to the hospital, I don't wear my uniform shirt. I took it and my vest off, then left it and my duty belt at the station.

Q. Did someone tell you not do that?

A. Yeah, but I felt more comfortable, because I obviously can't wear my gun, and I didn't want to be in uniform after all this without it.

So I take the shirt off and wear just my undershirt, pants, and boots, go to the hospital. While waiting to be treated in the waiting room, in the actual hospital room, the detective begins his interview, stopping as needed for the nurses, whoever came in. They take x-rays and prescribe a painkiller for the facial injuries.

St. Louis County's evidence technician arrives and photographs everything. I didn't know who he is, but he comes from whomever the department uses for drug tests, which they give me. After that, I think he leaves and the assistant chief drives me back to the station.

He had already made a phone call to have an officer provide a change of clothes for me, since they were going to take my clothes, as blood was on my left hip area.

So when I come back, I change. St. Louis County takes my pants and shirt, but they already have my weapon, so that was it. I went home for the day.

Q. Okay. You have been on administrative leave since then?

A. Correct.

Q. Okay. First of all, you have been a police officer for how long?

A. Five years.

Q. Any other incidents where you've been involved, where you had to use excessive force?

A. I've never used my weapon before.

Q. No excessive force, but have you had to use force to affect an arrest?

A. I've used my ASP and my flashlight before, as well as the OC spray.

Q. Okay. However, in those incidents, no one was injured?

A. No.

Q. Okay. All right.

Anyone else have any questions?

Grand Juror: I want to go back to when Sergeant [redacted] arrived there. You told him that you had to kill Michael Brown. Was that the extent of your conversation or did you tell him sort of like you are telling us, play-by-play, what happened?

A. No, it was very brief and he was more focused on the scene than he was, I guess, with me at that moment, because the crowd was not a good area. I made those comments to him and his reaction was to go sit down.

Grand Juror: If you would go back to the contact in the car, after you put it in reverse and reengage to have a conversation. Michael Brown reaches into the car with his right hand and you said at a certain point that you look in the mirror to see Dorian Johnson, because that's how you recognize him with his black shirt?

A. I do that before I place the car in reverse.

Grand Juror: Go over that again with me, which mirror are you looking at?

A.   My driver's side mirror on the outside of the car.

Grand Juror: Okay.

A.   Whenever they walked me and I saw the cigarillos, I'd already seen that Dorian Johnson had on a black shirt. However, just to double-check myself to match up with what I heard about cigarillos being stolen and the suspect was wearing a black shirt, I look to make sure the shirt was black.

Grand Juror: Okay.

A.   And then I call for an assist car, place it in reverse, and back up on him.

Q.   Ms. Alizadeh: Officer Wilson, I have a few questions. Prior to today, at any time after this incident, have you seen any reports of any kind, medical examiner's reports, police reports, hospital reports, or anything of that nature?

A.   The only report I've seen was the one released on the news about the initial stealing.

Q.   Okay. So that is the Ferguson report that was filed in relation to the theft of the cigarillos?

A.   Correct.

Q.   I'm guessing that the vehicle you were in is not equipped with any cameras or mics?

A.   No, it is not.

Q.   To record what was going on, correct?

A.   Correct.

Q.   Are any of the Ferguson officers' vehicles equipped with that type of equipment.

A.   No, ma'am.

Q.   Now, your duty holster that you've described or your duty belt has the holster attached to it, correct?

A.   Correct.

Q.   Is it the type of holster that has a snap that goes over the gun and you have to unsnap it before the gun is removed from the holster?

A. No, it doesn't have the strap on the top, but there is a button on the outside of it. You push it as you are pulling up and it releases it.

Q. Okay. And that is something that, I mean, as a police officer, you have to train at the firing range, is that fair to say?

A. Yes, ma'am.

Q. And is part of your training, learning how to quickly get your gun out of your holster?

A. Yes, ma'am.

Q. When you call in and say you have two on Canfield or two out, I think you say … ?

A. I say, "Frank 21, I'm on Canfield with two, send me another car."

Q. With two. And why didn't you say anything about asking again, what was the description of the two involved in the larceny? Did you ask for any other details to ensure in your own mind that maybe these were those guys?

A. No, because my initial focus was just to get the information out that I was there, have the other car respond, and then get to that. My whole goal was just to stall until someone got there.

Q. Well, you've made previous statements about that, this incident, and one being initially to your sergeant.

A. Uh-huh.

Q. Would you say that was a kind of brief, not a lot of detail statement, would that be fair to say?

A. The one on scene?

Q. On scene.

A. Yeah, that was very brief.

Q. And then you talk to Detective [redacted]?

A. Correct.

Q. At the hospital. And that was a little more detailed, would that be fair to say?

A. Yes.

Q. You didn't say anything about the cigarillos, did you?

A. Yes.

Q. You believe you did?

A. Yes, ma'am.

Q. Did you tell the detective that when you saw him with his left hand reaching back and he made the statement, here, hold these or whatever, that you saw what was in his hand?

A. I saw the flash of them going back behind him.

Q. So you didn't see at that point what was in his hand?

A. I could see the red and white wrapper of a cigarillo in his hand.

Q. Okay. Just so I can be sure I'm understanding you. Did you see that they were cigarillos?

A. I assumed they were cigarillos at that point. I saw that they were in his right hand before the contact was made.

Q. Did you ever grab ahold—you said that you grabbed ahold of his right hand at some point?

A. It was his forearm—it was this area (indicating).

Q. And what were you doing when you grabbed ahold of his right forearm?

A. Trying to move and somewhat control him, so I could get out of the car.

Q. Were you ever pulling him to try to pull him into the vehicle?

A. No, I was trying to open my car door with my left hand and then hold onto him as I did so.

Q. So you've got your left hand, but what's holding his right hand?

A. My right hand.

Q. And you are trying to open your door?

A. Yes.

Q. And this is before you've gone for your gun?

A. Yes.

Q. The first shot you've described in detail. I think I understand the first shot. The second shot you said you kind of weren't looking, I guess?

A. Yes.

Q. Where was your gun pointed?

A. His general direction.

Q. Was your gun above the level of the door frame?

A. I would say yes. It had come up and was not on my leg anymore. My leg sits only that far away from the top of the window, so I remember doing it like this, having my gun up.

Q. And you said you saw a little puff of dust or dirt that you assume was where the projectile might have landed in the dirt; is that correct?

A. Yes, ma'am.

Q. So your gun wasn't pointed like up in the air, would that be fair to say?

A. Yes, ma'am.

Q. Was your gun, if you had rolled up your window, let's just say, was your gun totally inside the vehicle, partially out of the vehicle, or was your hand extended so that the gun was totally outside the window?

A. I don't know for sure, but it was my right hand with it and it was ... I don't know where it could have gone.

Q. And at that point, Michael Brown is not right up on the vehicle, is that fair to say?

A. No, this is when he's coming back at the vehicle. He is only about a foot away and then after the first shot hit him, he went down and kind of held his hip for a second and then he came back up and started to come back in the vehicle. And that's when I just pulled the trigger.

Q. Did you give him any kind of warning before the second shot?

A. I don't recall.

Q. Ms. Whirley: You said you knew the area and you felt threatened in that, because there is violence and guns and everything, and that Michael Brown was being confrontational before the first blow, correct?

A. Yes.

Q. Is there any reason why you didn't wait in the car until your backup came?

A.   I thought I would be able to stall him until someone got there. I thought that if I could just get out of the car, I could maintain the distance that I needed to maintain until they were close. I figure all I needed was 20 or 30 seconds and someone is going to be there.

Q.   Right. So why wouldn't you stay in the car?

A.   Because I had already been, my comfort zone is not to be sitting in the car talking to someone else. I wanted to be out of the car, that way if I need to run I can run.

Q.   You can run?

A.   If I was out and he started like chasing me or went to hit me, I could move.

Q.   You are in a car, you are more mobile in a car than you are on foot, right?

A.   Right, but I also didn't want him to run away, so I needed to kind of stay where I can keep him there, yet keep myself safe while waiting for someone to get there.

Q.   Now, Officer Wilson, I'm not trying get in your head—I mean, I guess we all are trying to get in your head at some point to know what you were thinking at the time. However, I mean, your initial confrontation or your initial contact with them, I mean, you didn't see any of them with weapons, correct?

A.   No.

Q.   And they weren't subjects that you knew to be armed and dangerous?

A.   No.

Q.   And you stop and encounter pedestrians probably almost on a daily basis when you are on patrol, would that be fair to say?

A.   Yes.

Q.   And so did you at that point have any reason to anticipate that this, that Michael Brown, the Michael Brown subject was going to provoke or assault you?

A.   No, not at that moment, no.

Q.   You described the first shot, was his right hand on the gun when the shot went off?

A. I believe so.

Q. And then the second shot, was his body in contact with you on the second shot?

A. Probably not on the second one. I know when I first pulled the trigger, it was, but the gun didn't fire and then that's when I racked the gun and shot again.

Q. And you used both hands—you had to use both hands to rack the gun?

A. Yes, ma'am.

Q. Was he still trying to hit you when you went to rack the gun?

A. I didn't look up.

Q. Okay. So you said you did that without looking and then you just went like that?

A. Yes.

Q. Turned your face away and shot out the window?

A. Yes.

Q. In his general direction?

A. Yes.

Q. And so you can't really say whether his hands were inside the car or outside the car at the time you actually fired the second time, the second shot?

A. No, I can't tell you.

Q. The blood on your pants, do you know how the blood got on your pants?

A. No, I do not.

Q. Do you recall, I mean, when you were done and you noticed that you had blood on your left palm.

A. Yes.

Q. And the back of your right hand?

A. Yes.

Q. Did you wipe your palm on your pant leg, because it is on your left pant leg, correct?

A. Correct.

Q. Did you wipe your hand on your pant leg to get the blood off your palm?

A. Not that I remember. I didn't see the blood on my palm until I was driving back to the station.

Q. Okay. So you don't recall if you wiped the blood on your pants?

A. No, I don't.

Q. And at any time after you got back to the station and you went to the bathroom, was there a mirror in the bathroom?

A. Yes.

Q. Could you see any blood on your face?

A. No, I don't remember seeing any on my face.

Q. I would imagine that at some point in your training you have learned something about blood spatter and blood spray and so forth, is that right?

A. It is kind of common knowledge, but no official training on how it works.

Q. I know you're not an expert, but you know that can happen when you are in close range when someone is shot, correct?

A. Yes.

Q. That spray or splatter can get on you?

A. Yes.

Q. Did you ever see anything like that? Obviously, we have seized your clothing and what's on there is what's on there, but did you have any of that on your face or your forearms or anything like that?

A. I don't recall seeing it on my face. I remember looking, but I don't remember washing my face. I would say no, it was not on my face. When I washed my hands, I did wash up like halfway up my forearm just to make sure nothing was on me. I had seen it on my hands and I just started washing.

Q. You didn't wash your face then prior to going to the hospital?

A. No.

Q. Did anyone that you recall ever swab your face?

A. Not that I—no.

Grand Juror: When Michael Brown, I guess, I guess at the point where I want to say it was the second shot, I know this is kind of after the fact. You said he stepped back a little bit and then he came back in on you?

A. That was after the first shot.

Grand Juror: After the first shot?

A. Yes.

Grand Juror: Did you ever think about, I know your vehicle was running, did you ever just think about getting in that bad boy and drive away?

A. No, I didn't. My thought is I was still dealing with a threat at my car. You know, we're trained not to run away from a threat, but to deal with it and that is what I was doing. It never entered my mind to flee.

Grand Juror: Did you ever or do you recall grabbing Michael Brown by the throat?

A. Never touched his throat.

Grand Juror: Shoulder?

A. No. Only part of him I touched was his right forearm.

Grand Juror: When Michael Brown was running from you, after the shots were fired within the car and they both just disappeared and you had Michael Brown in focus, did you ever at any time fire with his back facing you?

A. No, I did not.

Grand Juror: When you asked him to halt, and he turned around and stopped running, at any point did you ever think that okay, maybe he doesn't have a gun, I need to stop shooting?

A. When he was running towards me?

Grand Juror: Throughout the whole process. You're in your car and someone, you're struggling, tugging back and forth, did you ever think that he had a gun right then and there and he could have used it at any time?

A. I wasn't thinking about that at the time. I was thinking about defending myself whenever he was hitting me in the car.

Q. Ms. Alizadeh: So kind of going on that as well. So the comment that you made to your sergeant when he got there at the scene was that you said, "Brown went for my gun, so I had to shoot him." I think that kind of goes along with that. Because I think when I hear someone say he went for my gun, if I literally take that comment, I would assume that someone literally went to your holster and tried to pull it out—either unholstering it or literally taking it from you.

In this instance, that was not the case. You had already unholstered and you were aiming at him. He essentially, in your point of view, deflected or pushed it towards you, but he did not at any point try to pull it from your holster—I guess that's my question.

A. He didn't pull it from my holster, but whenever it was visible to him, he took complete control of it. Whenever it was displayed to him, he twisted it around so my hand was no longer this way, it was bent this way (indicating) and it was dug into my hip. He had complete control of the weapon at that time.

Q. Was your hand still on it and your finger on the trigger?

A. Yes.

Q. Okay.

A. He was controlling where the gun was pointed, how it got there, and his finger was in the process of going on the trigger with mine.

Q. Okay.

A. I could feel his fingertips on my trigger trying to get in the trigger guard.

Q. And I guess to be fair about this, any time any law enforcement officer has asked to speak to you, you have willingly and voluntarily come in and been interviewed and answered all their questions, is that fair to say?

A. Yes, ma'am.

Q. And you have never been back to work at the Ferguson police department?

A. No, I have not.

Q. This happens in a matter of how many minutes or seconds by the time that you saw them walking down the street until Michael Brown is dead in the street?

A. I would say less than a minute.

Q. Now, you know, I know you've probably thought about this every day since it's happened, would that be fair to say?

A. Yes.

Q. Replayed this in your mind over and over again?

A. Yes.

Q. And do you think that after having really thought about this over time and basically you've had to tell this scenario a few times, do you think that perhaps there are any additional details that you may not have given initially? Do you think that's because you're just now remembering them, because you are putting so much thought into what happened, or do you think that are things that maybe you kind of imagined happened—you understand my question?

A. Yeah, just from what I have been told about the incident originally, is that you are supposed to have 72 hours before you are actually officially interviewed, recorded statement, and all of that. You tend to remember more through a couple sleep cycles than what you do as soon as it happens. In a traumatic event, a lot of details kind of come as one detail. I mean, from what I understand, there hasn't been really anything significant that's changed.

Q. So you think when you were testifying today, you said you kind of thought, had a thought process. As this chaotic scene is unfolding, do you recall actually in your mind processing this in the way you've described or is it just reactionary?

A. No, I remember it actually, I picture a use-of-force triangle in my head when this first happened and I was going through the progression of what I could do as far as the use-of-force continuum is concerned.

Q. That is something you learn in the police academy?

A. Yes, ma'am.

Q. Prior to this incident, had you ever had any contact with any of the county detectives that you've met throughout this investigation?

A. No, I have not.

Q. Any of the agents, FBI agents, or federal agents involved in their investigation?

A. No, I have not.

Q. You felt like your life was in jeopardy when you were sitting in the vehicle?

A. Yes.

Q. You felt like when you exited the vehicle and the interaction with Michael Brown, he was advancing towards you, you felt like your life was in jeopardy?

A. Yes.

Q. And use of deadly force was justified at that point in your opinion?

A. Yes.

Q. Ms. Whirley: I was just going, if we are sort of done with your questioning, is there something that we have not asked you that you want us to know or you think it is important for the jurors to consider regarding this incident?

A. One thing you guys haven't asked that has been asked of me in other interviews is, was he a threat—was Michael Brown a threat when he was running away? People asked why would you chase him, if he was running away now?

I had already called for assistance. If someone arrives and sees him running, another officer could go around the back half of the apartment complex and try to stop him. What would stop him from doing what he just did to me to him or worse, knowing he had already done it to one cop? And there he was—he still poised a threat, not only to me, but to anybody else that confronted him.

Q. Along those lines, you feel like as a police officer, it is your obligation to follow that suspect?

A. Yes.

All right. If that's it then.

END OF TESTIMONY

State of Missouri v. Darren Wilson

Grand Jury Volume VIII

September 30, 2014

Excerpts from a Canfield Green resident before the grand jury: After the confrontation at the police car and after Michael Brown is shot. This testimony involves the placement of Michael Brown's hands and his movement towards Ferguson police officer, Darren Wilson. Additionally, activities in and around Canfield Green apartments are addressed. This witness, interviewed by the St. Louis county police, homicide unit, on August 12, 2014. This interview is referred to during the course of this witness' testimony.

FOR THE STATE: **MS SHELIA WHIRLEY**

MS KATHI ALIZADEH

EXAMINATION

MS WHIRLEY:

Q. He (Brown) was bent forward, correct?

A. Uh-huh

Q. Is that a yes?

A. Yes.

Q. Okay. His arms were at his side at this point?

A. Right, right.

Q. He was moving toward the officer?

A. Right, very slowly and wobbly.

Q. And the officer said stop, right?

A. Right.

Q. At that point, Michael Brown hadn't stopped—is that correct?

A. It looks like he was falling. He was staggering, trying to stay up. Okay, he was shot, he was hurt. He was trying to keep up on his feet. He wasn't going toward the officer to try to get him. He was trying to stand up. He was trying to maintain himself, but you could see his body was giving out. And the angle his body was, when he told him to stop that last time when he's looking at him and that's when the comments were made, he's getting ready to kill him. And no sooner than they said that he was going like this, his body was coming like this, because he wasn't even looking and he fired. That's the only way he could have hit him in the head, the only way. He was already on the way down. Granted, he's a big boy, but he was hurt.

Q. And this is the point right before that, that final shot you refer to …

A. Right.

Q. Trying to tell him to stop?

A.   Right, right. I became very hysterical [redacted] who has never seen anything like this in her life. My sister-in-law is going berserk. My brother and I look, but we didn't even see the other officer, he had just moved away. Our focus, our focus is [redacted]. So when I got everybody to the apartment, got them calmed down, I came back out. I left and ran up the street, because I wanted to see what happened. Not what happened, but to see Michael Brown, you know, just some visible reason I wanted to see the body. As I got there and close, I saw his face, so I knew who it was.

Q.   You talked before about people started coming out from everywhere at that point?

A.   From everywhere.

Q.   Can you tell us about that, what was going on at that time?

A.   They all were running out. From my vantage point, I can see every apartment on the opposite side of the street. I couldn't tell if anybody was at the immediate apartment building where he was shot. I didn't see anyone at the apartments that are already in the back of the driveway where he was stopped, where the memorial is, on this side of the street in my sight. I can't see that other part.

Q.   Just tell us about when you went out there you mentioned people coming out from everywhere from the back of the complex.

A.   From the back of the complex, from everywhere.

Q.   And you talk about August 12th, the one reason you came forward is in your conscious you wanted to make sure the family got the truth about what really happened—that is why you came forward?

A.   Yes.

Q.   Were you were concerned about what other people were saying?

A.   You have to understand out there, they were looking for anything. The majority of the folks that came running from the other sides and the back, those three or four gentlemen that run up, they were saying that he had his hands up like this.

Q.   Like straight up in the air?

A.   Straight up in the air.

Q.   With his palms facing the officer?

A.   Yeah, we were standing, no. The gentleman that was besides us, the workers, no. We knew that. And then you could see, you have to understand the mentality of some of these young guys. They have nothing to do. If they can latch onto something, they embellish it, because they want something to do. This is something that gives them, okay, now we have something to do to get into this. I've lived in this area on and off for almost [redacted] years. The majority of these people do not work. All they do is sit around and get high all day. That's it, and just talk stupid. And they had that there, when we was standing there, someone at the top of the hill. I had to go back to my porch, because someone at the top of the hill had fired off some shots. The officers heard it and they started running, okay. Everyone on the other side of the street started pointing. "Where did it come from?" they asked, with everybody pointing. Two of these people, I had never seen before in my life in the whole time I've been out there. They came up, and said, "You all better not say nothing. You all snitching and all of this upset [redacted]."

Q.   They said this to you?

A.   They were talking and I was looking at the officers. I happened to turn when someone said like, "What, what?" You know, I was like saying, "Wait a minute," I said. "Turn around, but everybody was still doing this." But she and this other girl made a point to say something to [redacted].

Q.   About not snitching?

A.   Right.

Q.   Two females?

A.   Yeah, I'm like, "What?" And I told the girls, "I tell you what, you all used a very derogatory term—turn around. Everyone is pointing that way, you know." For three days, I had to deal with [redacted] because that shook [redacted] to the core, just not used to anything like that.

Q.   Can you explain this, what prompted these girls to come over to [redacted]?

A.   Because everybody was pointing, you know, when they heard the shot. I was pointing and shouting, "Where did it come from?" Right, but the thing was, the whole crowd was pointing up to the top of the hill. And I'm like, "Wait a minute," they single [redacted] out and he wasn't even pointing.

Q. I understand, okay.

A. Okay, so the thing is I live there, so when it comes to saying certain things, I've got to protect [redacted]—I don't care. I'm sorry for his family's loss, but I have a family and that's number one. We was scared for three weeks, she was scared.

Q. Let me ask you this, before whenever we were talking about people coming out and hands up in the air, you said there were workers nearby who were saying hands in the air?

A. No, no, no, they didn't say that.

Q. What did they say?

A. They said his arms were shoulder-length, just above his shoulders.

Q. People were coming out and saying all kind of things. And you talked about people talking about him having his hands straight up in the air, but you kind of said, "No, that's not what I saw."

A. Uh-huh. When I came after the shots were fired and everything else, I came back down because the crowd was big—it grew in a split second.

Q. All right. Let's back up a little bit then. When you came down there, are people saying things that you didn't see? How quickly after those last shots were fired was that happening? I mean, were people actually saying things like that?

A. After he hit the ground, I would say it took at least about a minute.

Q. That's when the crowd starts to gather, it was like in an instant?

A. In a minute, maybe 20 to 30 seconds, up to two to three minutes, is all it took for the crowd to become at least 70 or 80 people, it grew so quickly.

Q. Not just the crowd, but people talking about saying things that didn't happen?

A. Right, right, they start embellishing it when the stepfather showed up.

Q. The stepfather?

A. I later found out that he's the first one to appear. I didn't know it was the stepfather until a few minutes later when he approached.

Q. When you say they started embellishing, what did you hear?

A. Oh, the officer ran up behind him and shot him in the back.

Q. That's not true?

A. Not true.

Q. What else?

A. He had his hands straight up in the air, not true. Then some guy, I don't know who the heck he was, because I had never seen him before, he came out of the blue. He was coming out saying that Mike had approached the officer saying, "Oh my god," and he had his hands in the air telling him, "Don't shoot, don't shoot, don't shoot."

Q. And you said he (Brown) never uttered a word right?

A. Right. I said what I could hear.

Q. And you went on to say, that's when everyone come back and all of them started saying things like, oh, "He was on his knees."

A. Yeah.

Q. When he shot him, he was on his knees?

A. Not true.

Q. And then he came by and they said he was lying down and the officer came and shot him in the head.

A. That was false.

Q. None of those things happened?

A. None of those things happened, none of those things.

Q. You talk about the things, the crowd grew and the young guys out there saying things that were not true. August 12th, you said something about this, so I want to ask you about it. By living out there, if you go against what they are saying, you're thinking they might mess you up and go crazy. What do you mean by that?

A. They had it in their mindset of what happened. They're set. They are looking for a reason to explode, because they don't have anything to do.

Q.   Why look for a reason to explode?

A.   They got nothing else to do. They are running all day, they are drinking and getting high all day. We see this all the time. We have been on Canfield Green apartment management to get all the drugs out of there. North Winds got so bad, they put up gates, but when the gates went up, the crime went up. They're all walking around with their pants below their butts and everything else, no t-shirts on and they're so strong, they will stand right there in front of you and roll that stuff up.

Q.   Do you think that's the general feeling there, if someone says something to either us or the police and goes against what they want that they will go against them?

A.   I think now as it is getting longer in time, the majority of them in our neighborhood, my community, want the truth. It is those outside forces that are coming in. When they burned that thing down (memorial to Michael Brown) yesterday, 80 percent of the people were from the city, not from here. Cars were coming in, the parking lots were full. That lets me know this is not Canfield. This is not Ferguson.

Q.   You mention the burning down issue, the memorial?

A.   Yes.

Q.   Did you see that?

A.   Oh yes.

Q.   What did you see?

A.   The charcoal gray car pulled up beside it. By the time I reached my front doorstep, he gunned or she gunned it and the car peeled off. Next thing I know—whoosh!

Q.   It shot up?

A.   It just blew up and it wasn't no slow flame either, it just went whoosh.

Q.   You're talking about the memorial?

A.   Yes.

Q.   Did you see anybody go or do anything?

A.   I didn't see anybody. They could have done anything from the car window. They could have thrown something out the window. But that was definitely to me an accelerant, because the way it went up, it just went whoosh. It wasn't a slow burn. I mean, they're talking about a candle, but most of the stuff was wet.

Okay.

END OF EXAMINATION

State of Missouri v. Darren Wilson

Grand Jury Volume X

October 6, 2014

Excerpts from a Canfield Green resident before the grand jury. A circuit judge addresses the grand Jury regarding independent investigations.

FOR THE STATE: **MS KATHI ALIZADEH**
                                  MS SHELIA WHIRLEY

EXAMINATION

MS ALIZADEH:

Q.   Now this was a Saturday, a sunny day, so did you see people out and about?

A.   Um, yeah, I mean not a lot of people, but the victim, as we came in off Canfield, he and the other young man were walking in the street. And I said something to my husband in effect, "Why don't they just get on the sidewalk?"

Q.   Okay, so when you came around the curve, you could see them walking in the street.

A.   Uh-huh.

Q.   Just the two of them?

A.   Yes.

Q.   Okay. Anything else that you noticed about them that drew your attention?

A.   No, I mean, like I said, it was a Saturday morning. They was just walking in the street and I made a note to my husband, why don't they just walk on the sidewalk, and that was pretty much it. He didn't say anything, so I didn't say anything, but we didn't blow up what was happening. We just kind of went around and did what we needed to do.

Q.   And so after you parked your car, what's the first thing you noticed going on around here?

A.   Well, once we were going up the steps, the police car came down going towards West Florissant, and I said to my husband, "Oh, he's going to stop them and tell them to get on the sidewalk."

Q.   And what do the boys do?

A. They were just kinda standing there. The officer backed the car up, but it was at an angle and that's when we heard two gunshots inside the vehicle.

Q. He's going westbound and then he puts it in reverse, backs up, and he's at a little bit of an angle in the street?

A. Yes.

Q. Did you hear tires squealing or screeching or anything?

A. No, it wasn't like it was a chase or anything. I mean, he just, I mean, I don't know what happened. They exchanged words, I'm quite sure, and, you know, you just, I think he kind of whipped the car in reverse so it was at an angle.

Q. The first time the officer encountered the boys, were they on the driver's side of his car or the passenger side?

A. All the way around on the driver's side.

Q. Okay. So then after he comes back, reverses, and stops the car at an angle, what do you see—what happened between the boys and the police officer?

A. We just kind of heard the two gun shots and I told my husband, "Oh no, he's shooting! They're shooting!"

Q. Okay. So you hear two gunshots?

A. Uh-huh.

Q. Were they in close succession like boom, boom or was there a pause between the two of them?

A. Well, more like pop, pop.

Q. Okay. After you hear the two gunshots.

A. Uh-huh.

Q. What do you see happening at the officer's car?

A. That's when the victim started running away from the car and the person that was with him, he kind of disappeared. The victim kind of, when he came out from the driver's side, he kind of hid on the back side of the car and that's when he ran.

Q. Okay. So he's running now down Canfield?

A. Yes, ma'am.

Q. And can you tell at this point if he's injured?

A. Well, he ran this way and then kind of stopped and looked down at his hands. I'm assuming there was blood, but he looked down at his hands and then he turned back around and started going towards the police officer.

Q. What does the officer do?

A. Well, by that time, he's out of the car and he's kind of, I guess, chasing the victim.

Q. You saw him get out?

A. Yes, from the driver's side.

Q. And so at that point, could you see if he had a gun?

A. Yes, he had a gun.

Q. But was it down at his side, was he running?

A. He had both hands on the gun.

Q. Okay. And so, did you ever observe or hear the officer firing, as he was running after the victim?

A. Yes, I did.

Q. How many shots did you hear as he was moving towards the victim?

A. I'm going to say maybe three to four shots as they were, I guess, walking kind of towards each other.

Q. And then, Michael Brown stops and you said he looks at his hands?

A. Uh-huh.

Q. Could you see anything in his hands?

A. No.

Q. Okay. So did the officer fire his weapon at any time other than the car? Did he fire his weapon before the victim turns around?

A. No.

Q. So from the time the victim turns around, is the officer still moving towards him or has the officer stopped?

A. He stopped.

Q. He'd stopped?

A. Uh-huh.

Q. What were Michael Brown's hands doing as he's walking?

A. He is walking like this and he kept walking, and I asked my husband, "Why don't he stop?"

Q. Okay. Did you see him fall to his knees?

A. (Shakes head.)

Q. So he just...

A. He just kind of toppled over.

Q. And he went straight down. Did the officer continue to fire after he fell to the ground?

A. No, he just kind of stopped and kind of froze and just looked.

Court Addresses the Grand Jury

It is Monday, October 6th and I'm back in front of you mainly because I'm always thinking about you and I have a little bit of information that I want to share with you. And I hope what I'm here to say will also guide you.

Um, I received some information that some of you may have done independent investigations or some research, and I'm here to caution you about that.

Your job, as you know, when I told you when you started here will be to listen to the evidence that you're going to hear and then at some point, you're going to be deliberating.

It's very important that you all come to deliberate, that you are all considering the same evidence. You will have your thoughts about the evidence you've heard, you will each have your own opinions, but the very important thing to give the decision you make creditability and value is that you are all considering the same information and evidence.

And so, I'm here to caution you, do not go out and do independent research and investigation. If there is something you want, you tell the prosecutors. They will go and get that for you. And if they can't get it for you, they'll tell you why they can't get it.

Ask for anything you think you need to reach the decision you're going to be reaching, and I can't caution you enough about that.

I've told you this before, but I think of you often, because, like I told you at the beginning and I still tell you this, you are the face of the community. This decision is important, you are good people. You collectively are our St. Louis County, that's our community here.

You are the face of our community. Your decision will be the decision of the community, because you good people have listened to all of this evidence and then reached your decision. The decision you reach will be thoughtful, it will be thorough, and it will be based on as much evidence as you ask for and that can be brought to you.

And just so you are deliberating and talking back and forth, just so you know, you're thinking about the evidence. That's why it is so important that you not do this independent research, independent investigation.

So I'm going to ask you to please, if there's something you have, it has to be shared collectively. I'm going to ask you from this point forward, do not go forward and do anything independently. Ask the prosecutors for it.

I guess I've stated what I really wanted to say, but I have such faith in you. I think, no matter what the decision is, your decision is going to be the result of a well-thought out and conscientious approach to considering it. That's what is provided for you in the law. You're going through a very hard task at this time.

But when you go through that task, you should know at the end of the day, and I will know at the end of the day, you have done everything that is provided for under the law in our justice system when grand juries sit, and you have done everything that has been asked of you as a citizen of St. Louis County.

So my caution to you is, if there is anything you want, you tell the prosecutors, they will get you that information. And if they can't, they will tell you why, otherwise, ask them why. You are certainly free to do that.

But keep yourself safe too. I respect the law and I follow it—I'm following the law right through to the very end. And, um, I will answer questions that people have, because people are free to ask questions in our justice system.

If the press comes to me and asks me questions, I am going to follow the law in that regard. I believe I have followed the law up to this point with regards to any questions from the media. I will continue to do that, but when you do independent investigations, I worry that you may expose yourself to dangerous situations. It may lead to more problems than we could ever imagine.

So please keep your research and investigation here in this room. Also, please keep yourselves safe and know that you are the very good people of St. Louis County. We are lucky to have you in St. Louis County doing this very difficult job. Your collective decision, when you reach it, will be the final decision, no matter what it is.

So it is nice seeing you once again. Thank you for your very hard work. That's all I wanted to say, thank you.

End of Judge [redacted] statement

State of Missouri v. Darren Wilson

Grand Jury Volume XVI

October 27, 2014

Excerpts from the grand jury testimony of a Canfield Green resident. Testimony given after an interview with the FBI on August 16, 2014, one week after the shooting death of Michael Brown. This interview and the official autopsy reports are cited during this witness' testimony.

FOR THE STATE: **MS SHELIA WHIRLEY**

MS KATHI ALIZADEH

EXAMINATION

BY MS WHIRLEY

Q.   Okay. You know why you're here?

A.   Yes, I do.

Q.   About the Michael Brown shooting?

A.   That's correct.

Q.   Do you remember that morning, August the 9th—it was a Saturday, 2014?

A.   Clearly.

Q.   Clearly, good. Tell us what you remember about that morning.

A.   Okay. Basically I was sitting on my porch around 11-ish. Somewhere in there. And I heard a gunshot or two.

Q.   So one or two shots?

A.   Yeah, one or two. And it caught my attention because I'm sitting on my porch. And, uh, I seen to go right into it.

Q.   Go ahead.

A.   I seen the officer, as well as Mike Brown.

Q.   Yes?

A.   Okay. Mike Brown was running and I came further to my porch balcony because I couldn't believe it, you know. To see a police officer shooting at an individual on my street was kind of far-fetched for me to believe.

Q.   All right. So you saw Mike Brown running and the officer was chasing him shooting after him?

A.   The angle that I was in, I seen him in view after he came from this building, he came more clearer to me.

Q. You are talking about you were moving?

A. I wasn't in clear view of him until he came in view of chasing Mike Brown.

Q. Okay. When the officer came into view, for you, where were you?

A. I was on my porch.

Q. All right. And where was Mike Brown?

A. He was running east-bound.

Q. Where was the officer?

A. Not too far from, a little bit further, because I seen Mike Brown clear as day. And then, I started to see the officer as he was getting closer, but he didn't get that close.

Q. The officer is coming after him and you hear shots fired?

A. After the shot, I guess when it grazed him on his arm.

Q. Now, you're guessing, why are you guessing that?

A. Because I didn't know where he got shot at, I'm assuming he got shot.

Q. And you learned that later from news?

A. Autopsy. All I know is that he turned around after the gunshot went off.

Q. And what was the officer doing?

A. He had his gun raised. (indicating)

Q. What in your mind is going on?

A. I was discombobulated, I didn't know what was going on, because I seen this individual, like I said, running on my street, like what's going on.

Q. Did Mike Brown say anything?

A. Stop shooting me.

Q. Did you hear him say that?

A. Yes in the distance that I was at, because I think he was in pain based on the gunshots due to his body, because he was taking them.

Q. Okay. All right. So the total number of shots you heard that morning?

A. I'm going to say ten, that's it. I can't give you no more.

Q. You think ten. I know you have heard information—the news about the autopsy and where the shots were on his body, right?

A. Yes and no, because I did not listen to or look at a lot a news. I just—

Q. But you know some of the information, about where he received the shots?

A. Yes, yes.

Q. Okay. Now do you recall when you first talked to the police?

A. I did not talk to the police.

Q. Who did you talk to?

A. FBI.

Q. Do you recall when you first talked to the FBI?

A. Yes, I do.

Q. When was that?

A. It was the following Saturday they came to everybody's apartment and questioned individuals.

Q. So approximately a week after—

A. Somewhere like that.

Q. This occurred?

A. Yes, ma'am.

Q. And did you give them a statement?

A. Yes, I did.

Q. Okay. As you are telling us here today, I believe you did not see the initial—

A. No, I did not.

Q. … when he first made contact with the police officer?

A. No ma'am.

Q. Okay, you only saw it when the police officer was pursuing him east on Canfield Drive?

A. Yes, ma'am.

Q. And just to make sure I'm clear, were you hearing shots as Michael Brown's back was turned?

A. Yes, ma'am.

Q. So it would be reasonable to assume that he's shooting based on what you're telling us, that he's shooting at Mike Brown as he's running away?

A. Yes, ma'am.

Q. Initially, you thought he actually shot him in the back, right?

A. Initially.

Q. Before you knew where the shots were?

A. Exactly.

Q. You realized he wasn't shot in the back, does that make sense with what you saw?

A. Yes, it does, it makes sense, it does. It makes sense to coincide with what I thought.

Q. And tell me again why you believe that he was hit before he turned around? We now know he wasn't shot in the back. You said you believe he was shot in the back, why did you think he was hit before he turned around?

A. Because I heard gunshots, you know, I heard the gunshot and when he turned around, I figure he was hit. And he immediately submitted, subdued hisself like, okay, this is real, you know.

Q. You didn't see anything that gave you the impression that he was injured?

A. No, I did not. I didn't see no physical indication on his body whatsoever based on distance.

Q. Okay. Was it strange to you that he was walking towards the police officer?

A. He was ready to give hisself up.

Q. Now, you seen the movie clip—I call it movie, but it's a news clip— with the two construction workers?

A. Yes, ma'am.

Q. And there's someone saying, "He wasn't a fucking threat"?

A. That was my voice.

Q. You have seen this and you verified that's your voice?

A. That was my voice.

Q. Okay, now once he, well, you already said you didn't see him hit the ground?

A. No, I did not.

Q. So where do you go after—

A. After he's on the ground.

Q. I mean, you just hear, see him approaching the officer, the officer is still shooting, what do you do?

A. I get closer. I come off my porch. I walk and he's laying on the ground. After more shots go off.

Q. Did you see the officer shooting into Michael Brown's body as he lay on the ground?

A. No, I did not. I can assume that that happened.

Q. Did you see him get shot in the head?

A. No, I did not.

Q. Now, how did you make contact with the FBI?

A. They made contact with me.

Q. Okay, so they came to your apartment?

A. (Nods head)

Q. Okay. Now, when you initially talked to the FBI, and we've listened to your statements, or Kathi Alizadeh and I have, there is information in there that the officer was standing over him while he laid on the ground and finished him off?

A. You know, I said that out of an assumption based on me being where I'm from and that can be the only assumption that I have.

Q. You didn't see him hit the ground?

A. I didn't physically see none of that, because of the blind spot in which I'm located. My assumption and my common sense leads me to believe that's what occurred.

Q. Did you know police officer Darren Wilson?

A. No, I do not.

Q. All right. The first time you talked to the FBI, which was a week after this happened, you told them a story that had a bunch of lies, isn't that right?

A. A bunch of lies?

Q. Well, you told them that you saw the officer stand over Michael Brown and empty his clip into the body and finish him off, didn't you say that?

A. Well, you know, I did say that, but it was based on my assumption. Like I told her earlier, I'm not able to see the closure of the situation.

Q. You told them that you saw Michael Brown get shot in the back and that's not true is it?

A. That's not true, based on the autopsy coming out.

Q. But you told them—

A. Yeah, I told them that.

Q. You saw Michael Brown get shot in the back?

A. I didn't see no indication of where he was shot at based on me seeing what I seen.

Q. And you told them that you saw the officer within an arm's length of Michael Brown shoot him in the head and you didn't see that, did you?

A. Based on assumption.

Q. But you told them?

A. Yes, I did.

Q. You saw that?

A. Yes, I did tell them that based on assumption.

Q. And then you also told them that after Michael Brown was on the ground, the officer stood over him and emptied his clip into him and finished him off, you told them that you saw that?

A. Based on assumption again.

Q. But you didn't tell them that you were basing that on assumption, you told them that you saw that?

A. I told them in the second meeting with the FBI, we all sat down and it was solely based on assumption, because I'm not able to be at a point to where I'm not able to see. I told them based on assumption, if you see the report, it says based on assumption and my common sense, I wasn't physically there so, therefore, I can only assume what happened.

Q.   Well, okay, so I listened to your statement.

A.   You can read it.

Q.   In your first statement you didn't tell them that you were assuming that, you told them that that's what you saw?

A.   And that's what the second visit was for—to clarify the first recording.

Q.   So in the second interview, they told you that, by the time you gave the second interview, at that point you had seen on the news there was an autopsy.

A.   Once again, I did not look at the TV or listen to reports. I looked at the reports as far as knowing his autopsy; I looked at it once to verify my clarification for myself, because I did not know where initially the bullets landed.

Q.   Well, you changed your story in the second interview to say that when he was running away, the officer's shot actually grazed him in the arm.

A.   And that's what it did.

Q.   And you saw that?

A.   Based on the autopsy once again.

Q.   So you are basing this on, not your personal observation?

A.   Well—

Q.   –Let me finish my question.

A.   Okay.

Q.   So you are basing this on, not your personal observation, but on just things that you heard in the media?

A.   It is concrete once the autopsy come out. I can assume anything based on me looking, I don't know, I don't know where the bullets was landing.

Q.   Didn't you say in your second interview you admitted that those things you said you saw you really didn't see them and you were bas-ing it on what you had seen in the media?

A.   That was the truth based on the autopsy coming back. I don't have no knowledge of giving autopsy, so yeah.

Q.   So it was after you learned that the things that you said you saw couldn't of happened that way, then you changed your story about what you seen?

A.   Yeah, to coincide with what really happened.

Q.   So is what you're testifying about today what you really saw or are you basing your testimony today—

A.   I'm not—

Q.   —let me finish my question. Are you also basing your testimony to-day on things that you assumed?

A.   You know, it is not a thing of assumption, based on being in the posi-tion when it happened in the beginning, because I don't know where the bullets was flying to, I can only assume that they landed where they landed.

      And that wasn't the truth of the matter being that autopsy came out and gave clarity based on what I saw.

END OF EXAMINATION

State of Missouri v. Darren Wilson

Grand Jury Volume XVIII

November 3, 2014

FOR THE STATE: **MS SHELIA WHIRLEY**

                            MS KATHI ALIZADEH

Excerpts from grand jury witness 48. Testimony is contradicted by an interview given to the FBI. Reference is made to the prior interview during the course of his testimony.

Witness 48, after being duly sworn testified.

EXAMINATION

BY MS WHIRLEY

Q. Throughout this proceeding, we intend to refer to you as Witness Number 48, okay and you don't live in Canfield Green—is that correct?

A. No, I do not.

Q. Who are your parents?

A. [redacted]

Q. Okay. And your sister?

A. [redacted]

Q. And they were with you that day on August 9th, 2014?

A. Yes.

Q. Ms. Alizadeh: Okay. Is there anything else we needed? Let's go and get started.

Just so that we are clear on this, and we talked to you about not using your family's names, just call them Mom and Dad and Sister. We won't need to redact if you say my mom, my dad, my sister stuff like that, okay?

A. Okay

Q. Ms. Whirley: You know we are here regarding the Michael Brown shooting?

A. Yes.

Q. Did you know Michael Brown?

A. No, I did not.

Q. All right. And you know he was shot by an officer?

A. Yes.

Q. Did you know the officer?

A. No.

Q. Did you know, do you know the officer's name today?

A. No.

Q. Okay, all right. So let's talk about August the 9th, 2014. How did you start your day?

A. Um, I was hanging out with my parents at first, then my [redacted] asked me to bring something to [redacted], and I did.

Q. Now your [redacted], where does [redacted] live?

A. [redacted]

Q. All right. So where were you, about what time of day was it?

A. Like 12:15 p.m.

Q. Okay. And you were, what kind of car were you in?

A. A minivan.

Q. A minivan with your parents?

A. Yes.

Q. Okay. Did you have a pretty clear view of what was ahead?

A. Yes.

Q. Did you see the police car?

A. Yes, I seen the cruiser.

Q. Okay. Were there any cars ahead of you before you reached the police cruiser?

A. No, the only thing that was in front of us was the cruiser and Michael Brown, his back was towards us, standing up on the cruiser. It was like maybe a few inches from it.

Q. How close I should say were you to the cruiser?

A. There was enough space for at least like two cars.

Q. And which way was the cruiser, we will refer to it as cruiser, was it facing?

A. It was facing towards West Florissant.

Q. Now you mention Michael Brown. What was Michael Brown doing?

A. He was standing at the cruiser like in front of it. I really don't know what he was doing, but he had his hands at least waist high in front of him.

Q. Could you see his hands?

A. No.

Q. All right. How did you know his hands was at the waist?

A. Because if you see something from the back, you can tell that their hands are not dropped or up, you can see them in front of you.

Q. You didn't see them dropped or up?

A. Right.

Q. Okay. Did you notice the car moving and when I say moving, I don't mean driving, I mean like shaking or any motion to the car?

A. I'm not sure if the car was rocking or anything because I was having a conversation with my sister. And I didn't really notice what was going on until I heard the first two gun fires.

Q. All right. So you heard, you say two gunshots?

A. Yes.

Q. When you heard the two gunshots, where was Michael Brown at this time?

A. He was on the side of the police cruiser.

Q. The driver's side?

A. Right. At the driver's side and then that's when he took off running.

Q. You actually saw him take off running?

A. Yeah, we actually sat in the van and watched him run down the street and then he turned around and came back towards the officer.

Q. And what—

A. The officer hopped out of his cruiser and chased him down Canfield. They got like right about here and then Michael turned around and charged towards the officer. The police officer drew his gun and was like stop, stop, stop and then he shot him.

Q. Okay. When the officer got out of the car, was he running too?

A.   He was running behind Michael, he wasn't really close to him.

Q.   Did he shoot, well, you didn't see his gun, but did you hear the shots?

A.   No, he did not fire at Michael while he was running away from him.

Q.   Okay, so when did you see the officer's gun?

A.   I seen the officer's gun when Michael turned around and he was charging the officer.

Q.   Okay, when he was running, I think you said he was yelling, "Stop"?

A.   I heard him yell stop at least three times.

Q.   When was the first time you heard him yell stop?

A.   When he was chasing, when he was chasing down Canfield.

Q.   As he was chasing him, he was yelling, stop?

A.   Yes

Q.   Michael Brown turns around?

A.   And starts to run back towards the officer and the officer drew his gun and he pointed it at him. The officer was like, "Stop, stop," and he was like backing up.

Q.   The officer was backing up?

A.   Yes.

Q.   Can you demonstrate for us how Michael Brown was coming towards the officer?

A.   He was like charging towards the officer with his hands drawn up in a fist running towards him.

Q.   Come towards me?

A.   Almost like a football player.

Q.   And the officer, can you show me how the officer was going backwards?

A.   He had his gun drawn. He was like, "Stop!" He was backing up, he was like, "Stop," and he didn't, so he shot him three times.

Q.   Three times?

A.   He kept yelling stop and Michael kept coming towards him.

Q.   At this time they are, at this intersection—

A.   We're stopped.

Q.   But you could see?

A.   Yes. We was closer to the trees here (indicating).

Q.   Did you get out of the car at any time?

A.   No.

Q.   Any idea how far apart that is?

A.   No, but it's not that far.

Q.   Okay, at any time did it look like Michael Brown had anything in his hands?

A.   No.

Q.   Did you ever see his hands near his waist?

A.   No.

Q.   Did you ever see his hands raised up?

A.   No, he looked like he was going to raise his hands at one point, but he didn't. He just continued to run forward.

Q.   Okay, tell us what you mean, demonstrate what you mean he thought about it, looked like he thought about it?

A.   I mean like, he's running and then he like stopped, he put his hands up like this (demonstrating) and then he kind of brought them back down and started running.

Q.   Okay, that's when he charged towards the officer?

A.   He was already running, he was still in the process of running, should I say.

Q.   Did you ever hear Michael Brown say anything?

A.   No.

Q.   Any idea how many shots you heard total?

A.   At least eight or nine.

Q.   Okay. You heard two at the car then you—

A.   Then I heard three and then like four more shots, maybe like one or two more after that.

Q.   And all of these were when Michael Brown was charging the officer?

A.   Yes.

Q.   Now, did you ever see anyone with Michael Brown?

A.   Um, I seen a dude before all the shooting happened, there was a guy, thinner dude with Michael. He had on a black T-shirt and some gray jogging pants.

Q.   Okay.

A.   I really didn't get a good look at his face.

Q.   Tell us how his hair was?

A.   He had dreadlocks.

Q.   Was he at the police car too when you first noticed Michael Brown?

A.   I was behind him. I didn't see where he came from.

Q.   When you looked and saw Michael Brown at the police car, did you see him also?

A.   I didn't see him come up on the cruiser, but when the first two shots had been, he was like in the area behind the cruiser and he took off running alongside of building eighteen.

Q.   Okay. Now did you discuss what was happening with the people that were in the car with you?

A.   The only thing was, my mom was like, did they shoot him? I was like, yeah, they shot him. I was like, he just shot the fuck out of him, that was all that was really said.

Q.   Okay. So are you close with your parents?

A.   Yes.

Q.   After this happened, I know you said immediately after it happened your mom was like, made some kind of comment about, did they just shoot him or something, but afterwards, did you talk about what you saw with your family?

A.   No.

Q.   Never have?

A.   (Shakes head.) I mean, nothing really to talk about. Just seen somebody get shot, okay. I mean, it is tragic, but I didn't know him so I didn't have sympathy for what was going on. I felt like he brought it on himself, because if you are going to rob a place then fight with the officer, of course they're going to shoot you.

Q. So let me ask you a question. So those are things that you learned afterwards?

A. Uh-huh.

Q. When did you learn, if you remember, that Michael Brown had robbed the place?

A. I heard it on the news where they burned down the Quick Trip in Canfield.

Q. And in your statements, previously you used the word, 'charged.' You said that Michael Brown charged the officer?

A. That's right.

Q. Did you ever hear your mom or dad use the term, charged?

A. No.

Q. So that is a term you used that picked to describe what you saw?

A. Yeah.

Q. And you also said that the officer said, "Stop, stop, stop"?

A. Right.

Q. Do you recall if the windows were open or closed that day?

A. They were open.

Q. So you're saying you could hear him and when you said it for the grand jurors, you kind of just spoke it, "Stop, stop, stop." Is that how he said it?

A. No, he was yelling.

Q. You could hear it as he was yelling?

A. Yes.

Q. Did you hear anybody else yell or anybody else say anything?

A. No.

Q. Didn't ever hear Mike Brown say, "Don't shoot"?

A. No.

Q. Or nothing like that?

A. No.

Q.   Did you, did you see anybody else, and you also talked about the skinnier boy with the dreads, did you see anybody else around here?

A.   No.

Q.   What about other cars that were maybe behind the police car?

A.   There were no other cars on the street. There was no cars.

Q.   So you didn't see like a white Monte Carlo or any other cars that were behind the police car?

A.   No.

Q.   After the shooting, did you see a car drive up in the grass to drive around the police car to leave the apartment complex?

A.   No.

Q.   Are you saying you didn't see it or are you saying it didn't happen?

A.   I'm saying if it did happen, it had to be after we pulled away completely away from Canfield, because while we were there, it did not happen.

Q.   Was there ever a time in that van when you looked away or put your head down or ducked?

A.   No.

Q.   You never got down in the van once you heard the first shots?

A.   No.

Q.   Have you heard—

A.   I was too busy watching what was going on.

Q.   Have you heard gunshots before?

A.   All the time.

Q.   So when you heard those two gunshots, you immediately recognized them as gunshots?

A.   Yes.

Q.   Did you ever see the officer's hands or arms out of the driver's window?

A.   No.

Q.   Did you see his gun come out of the driver's window?

A. No.

Q. As far as Michael Brown was, did you see his body moving in any way or was he standing still?

A. He was just standing there. I don't think he was really moving like, nothing like that in front of the cruiser and then you see him take off running after the first two shots.

Q. All right. So now you're saying that you didn't want your mom to give your name to the police, is that because you didn't want to be involved or is there another reason?

A. Because I didn't want to be involved and I didn't want to be sitting here doing this.

Q. I understand. You're not the first person to say that. Did you have a discussion with your mom and dad about coming forward to talk to the police?

A. No, she just told me that she felt bad she didn't say nothing. And I was like, if you feel bad, then go say something. I didn't know she was going to tell y'all my name. Under oath, you've got to tell the truth.

END OF EXAMINATION

State of Missouri v. Darren Wilson

Grand Jury Volume XIX

November 4, 2014

FOR THE STATE: **MS SHELIA WHIRLEY**
                  MS KATHI ALIZADEH

Excerpts from Grand Jury Volume XIX centered on the testimony of a St. Louis county police forensic scientist specializing in the testing for and verification of DNA tests conducted at the St. Louis county police crime laboratory. Much of this testimony is redacted due to the scientific and technical nature of the DNA testing procedures.

EXAMINATION

MS WHIRLEY:

Q. Good afternoon. If you could introduce yourself to the grand jurors and spell your name for the court reporter, please?

A. My name is [redacted]

Q. What's your occupation?

A. DNA technical leader with the St Louis county police department crime laboratory.

Q. What do you do generally?

A. Generally, I perform the duties of a DNA analyst. So that involves processing evidence submitted to the lab for DNA testing. As the DNA technical leader, I have additional responsibilities, primarily to ensure that our DNA section maintains compliance with the FBI quality assurance standards that are required for DNA testing laboratories.

Q. Are you employed with the St. Louis county police department, is that correct?

A. That's correct.

Q. And how long have you been employed with them?

A. It will be four years in February.

Q. Did you do any other scientific work before?

A. Yes, previous to my work with St. Louis county, I was a biologist and a DNA analyst with the St. Louis metropolitan police department crime laboratory for just over six years.

Q. You have a total of what, is it ten years or more?

A. Approximately, yes.

Q. What type of work, tell us about your education?

A.   I have a bachelors' degree in biology, as well as a bachelor's degree in anthropology from the University of Missouri-Columbia. And then, I have a master's degree in biology from Washington University.

Q.   Now, approximately how many DNA cases have you worked?

A.   Approximately 1,400.

Q.   Okay. Can you tell us, a case comes to you, how does it start for you, a case?

A.   Sure. Generally evidence is collected from a scene. That evidence is submitted to the laboratory and a biologist obtains that evidence from the vault. They process it for whatever bodily fluids or potential DNA may be there.

They perform their testing and collect samples from the various areas of the items. They forward that to DNA, which is where I come in.

Q.   They forward it to you?

A.   Correct.

Q.   You are one of the DNA analysts?

A.   Correct.

Q.   And I want to get a little bit more general information out there, but before I go to ask those questions, I do want to specifically state that you worked the Michael Brown shooting case—is that correct?

A.   Yes.

Q.   And did you work this one in an expeditious fashion or any differently than any other case?

A.   It was worked just like any other case. But it was worked, I guess, as a priority.

Q.   Okay. Priority is a better way to put it. Why, do you know why it was made a priority?

A.   Due to the sensitive nature of the case.

Q.   Within the United States, all the information that's coming out, we are trying to get this completed, right?

A.   Yes.

Q.   I think you kind of told us what your responsibilities at the crime lab are, correct? Is there anything else you wanted to add to that?

A. Not that I can think of.

Q. Okay. And what is DNA? We are going to play a little film. Is this a good time to do it?

A. Yeah, that would be great.

At this point in the testimony a CD is viewed by the grand jurors. The presentation is technical in nature and goes into the various types of DNA testing: how it is submitted to the crime lab, processing and chain of custody.

The witness explains DNA secretions: sweat, blood, skin cells, and semen being the bodily fluids that contain DNA. Means of identification and the methodology used to arrive at a compared to number. Many times more that the entire population of the earth.

EXAMINATION CONTINUATION: MS WHIRLEY

Q. What else do you have?

A. All right.

Q. Q15, tell us about Q15, tell us about that.

A. Okay. Sure. So this sample was from a reddish brown stain on the upper left thigh of PO Wilson's uniform pants. DNA from Q15 are consistent with being a mixture of two or more individuals. This profile can be separated into a major male component profile and a minor contributor consistent with police officer Wilson. Michael Brown is the source of the major male component profile connected from Q15.

Q. So tell us about the weapon?

A. Okay. The DNA testing results obtained from Q19 are consistent with being a mixture of three or more individuals. This profile can be separated into a major mixture of two individuals with a trace contributor. Again, the trace contributor is inconclusive. Michael Brown and police officer Wilson are included as contributors in this major mix profile.

Q. So if his (Michael Brown's) DNA is on the gun and the car and the door of the car, there is no way you can tell us is it because he touched the gun or because his blood may have been on there or some portion, sweat, saliva, you can't tell us exactly how his DNA got on that gun?

A.   That's correct.

Q.   Okay. Go ahead.

A.   So Q1-1 was Michael Brown's T-shirt. I believe this is where [redacted] attempted to swab areas that did not appear to have blood staining. The DNA typing results obtained from Q1-1 are consistent with being a mixture of two more individuals. This profile can be separated into major component profile consistent with Michael Brown and one or more trace contributors. And then, again, there's limited genetic information from the trace component, so inclusionary statements can be made regarding this portion of the mixture.

However, police officer Wilson is excluded as a contributor to this mixture profile.

Q.   So to say the thing that we said earlier, none of those match Officer Wilson?

A.   Yes.

Q.   If one of two would have matched, you would have said what?

A.   It is possible that one or two did, but overall he (police officer Wilson) was excluded.

Q.   Anything else of evidentiary value that we missed?

A.   I think the only other items that we have discussed would be the swabs from Michael Brown's other portions of his body, his hands.

Grand Juror Question: So on Q1-1, the report talks about possible Police Officer Wilson grabbed the shirt of Michael Brown, from what you seen from the area that you tested, you didn't get enough markers to verify that—that's true. From what you've seen, you didn't get any of the police officer's DNA off that shirt?

A.   Correct.

Ms. Whirley: All right. Any questions, Kathi?

Ms. Alizadeh: No.

Ms. Whirley: Anybody else? Okay. I guess you asked them along the way, that was good. Okay, thank you very much.

End of Testimony

INDICTING A HAM SANDWICH

Ah yes, the old, "A grand jury can indict a ham sandwich."

A term that caught on after Sol Wachtler, former chief judge of the New York Court of Appeals indicted on charges of extortion, racketeering, and blackmail. From his protestation of innocence he coined the term … "A grand jury can indict a ham sandwich."

The facts of the case involve the former jurist harassing a past lover, by sending sexually explicit letters, threatening notes, and eventually vowing to kidnap his previous paramour's daughter. Unbeknownst to the judge, the daughter's phone, monitored by the FBI, captured several calls that put "His Honor" in an unflattering and felonious light.

Indictment by a federal grand jury in Newark, New Jersey, followed. Indicted after the facts and circumstances were presented to the sitting grand jury—mere statements of another scoundrel, wrapping himself in the justice system and by proxy, the flag. All this after having served in the same system and should have, at least, a working knowledge of a grand jury system.

In the end after all the high-sounding, self-serving comments, former judge Wachtler pled guilty, forced to resign from the bench, and served a fifteen month prison term.

Another reason to indict a ham sandwich is, of course, when a ham sandwich commits an indictable offense.

Statement of St. Louis County
Prosecuting Attorney, Robert McCulloch

Grand Jury Results

November 24, 2014

First and foremost, I would like to extend my deepest sympathies to the family of Michael Brown. As I have said in the past, I know that regardless of the circumstances here, they lost a loved one to violence. I know the pain that accompanies such loss knows no bounds.

On August 9, Michael Brown was shot and killed by Police Officer Darren Wilson. Within minutes, various accounts of the incident began appearing on social media. The town was filled with speculation and little, if any, solid accurate information. Almost immediately, anger began brewing because of the various descriptions of what happened and because of the underlying tensions between the police department and a significant part of the neighborhood. The St. Louis county police conducted an extensive investigation of the crime scene, under trying circumstances and interrupted by gunfire on several occasions. Continuing after that, they, along with the agents of the FBI, at the direction of Attorney General Eric Holder, located numerous individuals and gathered additional evidence and information.

Fully aware of the unfounded but growing concern in some parts of the community that the investigation and review of the tragic death might not be fair, I decided immediately that all of the evidence gathered, all people claiming to have witnessed any part of the shooting, and all other related matters would be presented to the grand jury. Therefore, a judge selected

12 members of this community in May of this year long before the shooting occurred.

I would like to expand briefly upon the unprecedented cooperation of the local and federal authorities. When Attorney General Holder first announced the investigation just days after the shooting, he pledged that federal investigators would be working with local authorities as closely as possible every step of the way and would follow the facts with no preconceived notion of where that journey would take us. The only goal was that our investigation would be thorough and complete to give the grand jury, the Department of Justice, and ultimately, the public all available evidence to make an informed decision.

All evidence obtained by federal authorities was immediately shared with St. Louis county investigators. All evidence gathered by St. Louis county police was immediately shared with federal investigators. Additionally, the Department of Justice conducted its own examination of evidence and performed its own autopsy. Another autopsy was performed at the request of the Brown family and this information was also shared. Just as importantly, all testimony before the grand jury was immediately provided to the Department of Justice.

Although the investigations are separate, both the local and federal government have all of the same information and evidence. Our investigation and presentation of the evidence of the grand jury has been completed.

The most significant challenge encountered in this investigation has been the 24-hour news cycle and the sensational appetite for something to talk about. Following closely behind were the rumors on social media.

I recognize the lack of accurate detail surrounding the shooting frustrates the media and the general public and has bred suspicion among those already stressed out by the system.

The most closely guarded details give law enforcement a yardstick to measure the truthfulness of what people said. Eyewitness accounts must always be challenged and compared against the physical evidence. Many witnesses to the shooting of Michael Brown made statements inconsistent with other statements they made and also conflicted with the physical evidence. Some were completely refuted by the physical evidence.

An example—before the result of an autopsy was released, witnesses claim they saw Officer Wilson stand over Michael Brown and fire many rounds into his back. Others claim that Officer Wilson shot Mr. Brown in the back as Mr. Brown was running away. However, once the autopsy was made public, it revealed that Mr. Brown had not been shot in the back or sustained any wounds to the back whatsoever. Several "eyewitnesses" adjusted their stories in their subsequent statements.

Some even admitted they did not witness the event at all, but merely repeated what they heard in the neighborhood or assumed. Fortunately for the integrity of our investigation, almost all of the initial witness interviews, including those of Officer Wilson, were recorded. The statements in the testimony of most of the witnesses were presented to the grand jury before the autopsy results were released by the media, and before several media outlets published information from reports they received from a DC official.

The jurors were, therefore, prior to the release of the information being made public and what followed in the news cycle—the jurors were able to assess the creditability of the witnesses, including those witnesses who statements and testimony remained consistent throughout every interview and were consistent with the physical evidence.

My assistants began presenting to the grand jury on August 23rd. The evidence was presented in an organized and orderly manner. The jurors gave us a schedule of when they could meet. All 12 jurors were present for every session and heard every word of testimony and examined every item of evidence.

Beginning August 20th and continuing until today, the grand jury worked tirelessly to examine and re-examine all of the testimony of the witnesses and all of the physical evidence. They were extremely engaged in the process, asking questions of every witness, requesting specific witnesses, requesting specific information, and asking for certain physical evidence. They met on 25 separate days in the last three months, heard more than 70 hours of testimony from about 60 witnesses and reviewed hours and hours of recordings of the media and law enforcement interviews by many of the witnesses who testified. They heard from three medical examiners and experts on blood, DNA, toxicology, firearms, and drug analysis. They examined hundreds of photographs, some of which they asked to be taken. They examined various pieces of physical evidence. They were presented with five indictments ranging from murder in the first degree to involuntary manslaughter. Their burden was to determine, based upon all of the evidence, if probable cause existed to believe that a crime was committed and that Darren Wilson was the person to commit the crime.

There is no question that Darren Wilson caused the death of Michael Brown by shooting him, but the inquiry does not end there. The law authorizes a law enforcement officer to use deadly force in certain situations. The grand jury considered whether Wilson was the initial aggressor in this case, whether there was probable cause to believe that Darren Wilson was authorized as a law enforcement officer to use deadly force in this situation, or if he acted in self-defense.

I detail this for two reasons: first so that everybody will know that, as promised by Attorney General Holder and me, there was a full presentation of all the evidence and appropriate instruction in the law to the grand jury. Second, as a caution to those in and out of the media who will pounce on a single sentence or witness and decide what should have happened in this case based on that tiny bit of information.

The duty of the grand jury is to separate fact from fiction, after a full and impartial examination of all the evidence involved, and decide if evidence supported the filing of any criminal charges against Darren Wilson. They accepted and completed this monumental responsibility in a conscientious and expeditious manner.

It is important to note here, and I say again, that they are only people, the only people who have heard and examined every witness and every piece of evidence. They discussed and debated the evidence among themselves before arriving at their collective decision. After their exhaustive review, the grand jury deliberated and made their final decision. They determined that no probable cause exists on any charges against Officer Darren Wilson and returned a "No True Bill" on each of the five indictments.

The physical and scientific evidence examined by the grand jury, combined with the witness statements supported and substantiated by the physical evidence, tells the accurate and tragic story of what happened.

The very general synopsis of the testimony and the physical evidence presented to the grand jury, with some exceptions, and the testimony of the witnesses called to the grand jury will be released at the conclusion of this statement.

At approximately 11:45 a.m. on Saturday, the 9th of August, Ferguson police officer Darren Wilson was dispatched to the Northwinds apartment complex for an emergency involving a two-month-old infant having trouble breathing. At approximately 11:53 a.m., while still at the Northwinds call, Wilson heard a radio call of a stealing in progress at a market on West Florissant. The broadcast included a brief description of the suspect: a black male, wearing a white t-shirt, who took a box of Swisher cigars. Officer Wilson remained with the mother and the infant until EMS arrived. Officer Wilson left the apartment complex in his police vehicle, a Chevy Tahoe SUV, and drove west on Canfield towards West Florissant. An additional description of the suspect was released at that time: wearing a red hat, yellow socks, and khaki shorts, and he was with another male.

As Officer Wilson was attending to his emergency call, Michael Brown and a companion were in the local convenience store. Michael Brown's activity in the store was recorded by the store security cameras. The video, often played following its release in August by the Ferguson police department, shows Michael Brown grabbing a handful of cigarillos and heading towards the exit without paying. As Michael Brown and his companion left the store, someone inside the store called the police.

Wilson observed that Michael Brown had cigarillos in his hand and was wearing a red hat. At approximately 12:02 p.m., Wilson radioed he had two individuals on Canfield and needed assistance. Officer Wilson backed his vehicle at an angle blocking their path and blocking the flow of traffic in both directions. Several cars approached from both the east and west, but weren't able to pass the vehicle.

An altercation took place with Officer Wilson seated inside the vehicle and Mr. Brown standing at the driver's window. During the altercation, Officer Wilson fired two shots, while still inside the vehicle. Mr. Brown ran east and Officer Wilson gave chase. Near the corner of Canfield and Coppercreek, Mr. Brown stopped and turned back towards Officer Wilson. Officer Wilson also stopped. As Michael Brown moved towards Officer Wilson, the officer fired several more shots and Michael Brown was fatally wounded.

Within seconds of the final shot, the assist cars arrived, less than 90 seconds passed between the first contact and the arrival of the assist car.

During the investigation, the media interviewed eyewitnesses—by various news outlets. Local and federal law enforcement interviewed witnesses, sometimes together and sometimes separately. All the statements were provided to the other party. All previous statements of witnesses who testified before the grand jury were also presented to the grand jury whether they were media interviews or interviews by the FBI or by the county police department.

The statements of all witnesses, civilian, law-enforcement, and experts were challenged in court by other law-enforcement, by the grand jurors, and the prosecutors. A common and highly effective method for challenging a statement is to compare it to the previous statements of the witness for consistency and to compare it with the physical evidence.

The physical evidence does not change because of public pressure or personal agenda. Physical evidence does not look away as events unfold nor does it black out or add to memory. It remains constant and is a solid foundation upon which cases are built.

When statements changed, witnesses were confronted with the inconsistencies and conflict between their statements and the physical evidence. Some witnesses admitted they did not actually see the shooting or only saw part of the shooting, only repeating what they heard on the street. Some others adjusted parts of their statements to fit the facts. Others stood by original statements even though their statements were completely discredited by the physical evidence. Several witnesses describe seeing an altercation in the car between Mr. Brown and Officer Wilson. It was described as a tug-of-war. Several witnesses described Mr. Brown as punching Officer Wilson while Mr. Brown was partially inside the vehicle. At least one witness said no part of Mr. Brown was ever inside the vehicle and that the shot was fired through an open window while Mr. Brown was standing outside.

Various technicians and scientists examined the vehicle, Officer Wilson's clothing, and equipment. Mr. Brown's blood and DNA were located on the outside of the driver's door. His blood and DNA were found on the outside of the left-rear passenger's door. Mr. Brown's blood and DNA were found on the inside of the driver's door, the upper-left thigh of Officer Wilson's pant leg, the front of Officer Wilson's shirt, and on Officer Wilson's weapon. Additionally found, a bullet fired from inside the vehicle striking the door in a downward angle at the armrest. The second bullet was not recovered.

Regarding the gunshot wounds of Mr. Brown, it should be noted that three separate autopsies were conducted—one by the St. Louis medical examiner, one by a private pathologist, and one by the Department of Defense. The result of all three autopsies were consistent with one another in all significant respects. Mr. Brown had a gunshot graze wound on his right hand, on his right thumb. The path of the bullet was away from the tip of the hand. Soot consistent with a close range gunshot was present in that wound. Officer Wilson also had a medical examination, which indicated some swelling and redness to his face.

Almost all witnesses stated that after they heard the shots fired while Mr. Brown was at the car, he hesitated and then ran east. Most stated that almost immediately, Officer Wilson got out of his vehicle and chased after him. Some witnesses stated that Wilson fired at Mr. Brown as he chased after him, striking him. At least one witness said one of the shots struck Mr. Brown. Others stated he did not fire until Mr. Brown turned and came back towards the officer.

At least one witness stated that, as Officer Wilson got out of his vehicle, he shot Mr. Brown multiple times, as Mr. Brown stood next to the vehicle. Yet another witness stated that the Officer Wilson stuck his gun outside the window and fired at Mr. Brown as Mr. Brown was running. One witness stated there were actually two police vehicles.

Most witnesses agreed that near the corner of Canfield and Coppercreek, Mr. Brown stopped and turned around, facing Officer Wilson. Some said Mr. Brown did not move towards Officer Wilson at all, but was shot multiple times as he stood near the corner with his hands raised. In subsequent interviews with law enforcement or other testimony before the grand jury, many of the same witnesses said they did not actually see the shooting. Some were running for cover, some were relating what they had heard from others, or they said what they assumed happened in that case.

Several other witnesses maintained their original statement that Mr. Brown had his hands in the air and was not moving towards the officer when he was shot—excuse me—several witnesses stated Mr. Brown did not raise his hands at all or that he raised them briefly and then dropped them and turned towards Officer Wilson, who fired several rounds. Other witnesses stated Mr. Brown stopped for a very brief period and then began to move towards Officer Wilson again. One describes his movement as a "full charge."

According to some witnesses, Officer Wilson stopped firing when Mr.

Brown stopped moving towards him, and returned firing when Mr. Brown started moving towards him again. These witnesses did not make statements to the media.

The descriptions of how Mr. Brown's hands were raised, raising his hands, or the position of his hands is not consistent with the witnesses. Some describe his hands being out to his sides, some said in front of him with palms up, others said his hands were raised up by his head or by his shoulders. Still others describe his hands as being in the running position or fists.

There are also various witness statements regarding Mr. Brown's movement after he stopped and turned back towards Officer Wilson. Several witnesses said Mr. Brown never moved towards Officer Wilson when he was shot. Most said the shots were fired as he moved towards Officer Wilson. Mr. Brown's movements were described as "walking," "moving fast," "stumbling," or "full charge." The varying descriptions were sometimes provided by the same witnesses in subsequent statements for testimony.

The entire area was processed by the St. Louis county crime scene unit. Officer Wilson fired a total of twelve rounds—two at the car and ten more farther east.

Mr. Brown sustained a graze wound to his thumb while standing next to the vehicle. He sustained six or seven more gunshot wounds, depending upon whether one of the shots was an entry or reentry wound; Mr. Brown sustained a second graze wound, another graze wound to his right bicep. He also sustained wounds to his right forearm, upper-front right arm, lateral-right chest, upper-right chest, forehead, and top of the head.

The top of the head, forehead, and perhaps the upper-right chest were consistent with his body being bent forward at the waist. Except for the first and last wound, the medical examiners were unable to determine the order of the shots. The graze wound of the thumb sustained at the vehicle was likely the first wound. It was the only close range shot. The shot at the top of the head was most likely the last. It would've rendered him immediately unconscious and incapacitated.

Mr. Brown's body was located approximately 153 feet east of Officer Wilson's car. Mr. Brown's blood was located approximately 25 feet farther east, past his body. A nearby tenant during a video chat inadvertently captured the final ten shots—ten shots on tape. There was a string of shots, followed by a brief pause, and then another string of shots.

As I stated earlier, the evidence and the testimony will be released following the statement.

I am ever mindful that this decision will be accepted by some and may cause disappointment for others. All decisions in the criminal justice system must be determined by the physical and scientific evidence, and the credible testimony corroborated by that evidence—not a response to public outcry. Decisions on a matter as serious as charging an individual with a crime cannot be decided upon anything less than complete examination of all available evidence. Anything less is not justice. It is my sworn duty and that of the grand jury to seek justice, and not simply obtain an indictment or conviction.

I do want to say that during the course of this extremely tense and painful time that we have, the citizens of this community should be, and are, very mindful of the fact that the whole world is watching to see how we respond and how we react. I would urge each and every one of them to remember the loss suffered by the Brown family—no young man should ever die so needlessly.

This is a loss of life, and it is a tragic loss, regardless of the circumstances. But it opens old wounds and gives an opportunity now to address those wounds as opposed to in the past, where they just fade away.

How many years have we talked about the issues that lead to incidents like this? And yet, after a period of time, it just fades away. I urge everyone who was engaged in the conversation, who was engaged in the demonstrations, to keep that going and to do it in a constructive way, a way we can profit from this. One way we can benefit from this is by changing the structure, and changing some of the issues, by resolving the issues that lead to these sorts of things.

I join with Michael Brown's family, and with the clergy, and with anyone else; the NAACP, the Urban League, and every government official, and private citizen that you've heard encouraging everyone to continue the discussion, continue the demonstrations, address the problems, but to do so in a constructive, not destructive way.

AFTER THE GRAND JURY DECISION

The prosecuting attorney for St. Louis County, on November 24th, 2014, announced that former police officer Darren Wilson would not be indicted on any charges resulting from the shooting of Michael Brown, Jr. on August 9, 2014.

A crowd of about 350 protesters, some peaceful and some not so peaceful, gathered on West Florissant Avenue in Ferguson. Media were poised, like a shark smelling blood, cameras at the ready. The trucks with labels, CBS, NBC, Al-Jazeera lined the street.

Lesley McFadden and her current man of the hour, Louis Head, stood on a car hood. Head screamed at the crowd, "Burn this bitch down, burn this Muthafucker down!"

President Obama came out with a weak, limp-wristed response to the grand jury decision, "This is not a reason for violence." He prefaced this statement by a general statement indicating that Ferguson is like many communities throughout the country where police are racists.

Isn't that getting a little old?

The president said, "...there are Americans who agree with it, and there are some Americans who are deeply disappointed, even angry. It is an understandable reaction ... As they (police) do their jobs in the coming days, they need to work with the community, not against it ..."

"Finally, we need to recognize that the situation in Ferguson speaks to a broader challenge that we still face as a nation. The fact is, in too many parts of the country, a deep distrust exists between law enforcement and communities of color. Some of this is a result of the legacy of racial discrimination in this country—and this is tragic—but also those who are interested in working with this administration, local, and state officials, to start tackling much-needed criminal justice reform."

"But what is also true is that there are still problems and communities of color aren't just making these problems up. Separating that from this particular decision, there are issues in which the law too often feels as if it is being applied in discriminatory fashion. I don't think that's the norm. I don't think that's true for the majority of communities or the vast majority of law enforcement officials. But these are real issues. And we have to lift them up and not deny them or try to tamp them down. What we need to do is to understand them and figure out how do we make more progress. And that can be done."

" ... Michael Brown's parents understand what it means to be constructive. The vast majority of peaceful protesters, they understand as well."

Did our president not see Michael Brown's mother and stepfather inciting the already electrified crowd to "burn this bitch down?"

"And I am confident that if we focus our attention on the problem and we look at what has happened in communities around the country effectively, then we can make progress not just in Ferguson, but in communities around the country."

What? Our president had the opportunity to use his God-given skills and talents as an effective and forceful orator to offer a more soothing and calming voice to this volatile situation. Could not the president, being a lawyer, address briefly the concept and need for probable cause? In this case, none existed, but then, perhaps the audience would fail to grasp the notion of laws based on reasonableness—not emotion. He could have easily asked for calm and cool heads to prevail or called upon clergy and community leaders to instill a sense of peace and respect for the rule of law. He missed an excellent opportunity to soothe a wounded nation, as the Department of Justice would soon disseminate, " ... a tense and emotional time, built on false conclusions, testimony and a rush to judgment by many news outlets." Shouldn't news institutions report the news, not make it up? This kind of reporting is what fans the flames of a perceived grave injustice.

Our president knew or should have known about the false accusations, deceptive and untruthful actions that led to the protests turning violent.

Large, angry crowds in major metro areas were ready to spring as they awaited the announcement of the grand jury findings. All they needed was just a spark, an excuse to begin days of violence. However, all this could have been avoided or at least subdued, if Mr. Obama had leveled with his countrymen and gave a truthful account of what really occurred.

This from a president who promised to bring the country together as one—white, black, or brown. Another empty and failed statement. Race relations have never been worse.

Our president is doing nothing to bring everyone together. Just the opposite. Recalling Jim Crow laws, slavery, and the brutality of Christians. These are in the past. Let's look forward to a future where all can share in the American dream. Mr.President, really!

THUGS?

At first glance, maybe. Then again, maybe not. In this case, no, hell no!

These men, tired of all the negative press and coverage of the Ferguson shooting and its aftermath, decided to do something about it.

According to news reports, the four black men who stood outside the Conoco gas station on West Florissant Avenue took it upon themselves to stand guard in front of the station. These men undertook this action to prevent it from being overrun and looted by those predisposed to engage in criminal activity. One of the four, the holder of a concealed carry permit, brandished a .40 caliber pistol. When approached by a group intent on looting the store advised the would-be felons, "This is not the place to steal from ... "

It is interesting to note that the owner did not pay or compensate the guardians. The business has been in the family for three generations. One of the protectors, when questioned by a local reporter asked, "Why are you protecting a business owned by a white man?"

"Why, because the owner is a good person. He has treated us fairly and with respect. He has provided employment and educational opportunities for a number of kids, that's why." Stupid question, excellent answer from a cool, levelheaded resident of Ferguson.

A drive along West Florissant Avenue reveals businesses to the north and south of the Conoco station torched and left in ruin. One could opine that the burned and abandoned locations, which were once tax-generating operations, will never be rebuilt. Never to, once again, provide employment opportunities to those most in need of gainful jobs. Most in need of the dignity and respect that comes from earning a wage in return for your labors.

The actions of these residents are in deep contrast to those that, under the guise of being peaceful protesters, continue to harass and assault police officers attempting to maintain the peace.

Perhaps one of the most egregious acts was when a group of 10 to 15 outraged demonstrators taunted two black female police officers by repeatedly calling them, "House Niggers." These demonstrators should be ashamed of themselves. They probably aren't, but they should be.

Another deplorable action was when protesters flashed lasers at the eyes of a police officer standing on the line. The officer instinctively raised his shield and took a stance in what he perceived to be an attack. The numerous TV cameras immediately focused on the officer. A stern-faced reporter explained that this is yet another attempt by the police to cause the "peaceful protester" to take action against this offensive move by police.

US ATTORNEY GENERAL ON THE RESULTS OF THE ST. LOUIS COUNTY GRAND JURY

Eric Holder released the following statement regarding the St. Louis County grand jury decision on November 24th regarding the shooting of Michael Brown, Jr. by Ferguson police officer Darren Wilson:

"While the grand jury proceedings in St. Louis County has concluded, the justice department's investigation into the shooting of Michael Brown remains ongoing. Though we have shared information with local prosecutors during the course of our investigation, the federal inquiry has been independent of the local one from the start and remains so now. Even at this mature stage of the investigation, we have avoided prejudging any of the evidence. And although federal civil rights law imposes a high legal bar in these types of cases, we have resisted forming a premature conclusion."

"Michael Brown's death was a tragedy. This incident has sparked a national conversation about the need to ensure confidence between law enforcement and the communities they protect and serve. While constructive efforts are underway in Ferguson and communities nationwide, far more must be done to create enduring trust. The department will continue to work with law enforcement, civil rights, and faith and community leaders across the country to foster effective relationships between law enforcement and the communities they serve and to improve fairness in the criminal justice system overall. In addition, the department continues to investigate allegations of unconstitutional policing patterns or practices by the Ferguson police department."

"Though there will be disagreement with the grand jury's decision not to indict, this feeling should not lead to violence. Those who decide to participate in demonstrations should remember the wishes of Michael Brown's parents, who have asked that remembrances of their son be conducted peacefully. It does not honor his memory to engage in violence or looting. In the coming days, it will likewise be important for local law enforcement authorities to respect the rights of demonstrators, and de-escalate tensions by avoiding displays—and uses—of force."

Really? This reads like a "White Paper" on policing in America. Once again, like our president, Holder missed an excellent opportunity to ask for calm and reason during these trying times. Mr. Holder must have known or damn sure should have known about the "Hands up, don't shoot," being bogus at the time of the grand jury decision. As stated on page 83 of the Department of Justice memorandum titled "DEPARTMENT OF JUSTICE REPORT REGARDING THE CRIMINAL INVESTIGATION INTO THE SHOOTING DEATH OF MICHAEL BROWN BY FERGUSON, MISSOURI POLICE OFFICER DARREN WILSON," dated March 4, 2015.

This is November 23, 2014—two-and-a-half months after the shooting incident. Mr. Holder stated above, " ... even at this mature stage of the investigation ... " Our attorney general had to have the facts and circumstances of the incident. The false and misleading testimony of witnesses. The DNA evidence. The results of the three autopsies. All the country needed at this time is the truth. Something our nation's leaders have sworn to uphold.

Sadly, the truth of this incident did not reach the people of the United States and the world stage until the release of the Department of Justice investigation into the shooting of Michael Brown, Jr. on March 4, 2015.

Upon the release of the shooting incident, a DOJ report on the Ferguson police department was also released. The focus our leaders took, not to advise the nation that the premise of the "hands up, don't shoot," and of the lawful use of force by a police officer. Oh no, the focus is placed on the "racist" Ferguson police department. It is interesting to note that much of the "evidence" obtained by the DOJ is classified as "anecdotal," or not confirmed.

How can this be? The DOJ report must deal with facts. Not anecdotal. Stories spun by individuals off the street who may or may not have been residents of the city of Ferguson. We deserve better.

Once again, Mr. Holder missed another excellent opportunity to sooth the country by announcing the findings of the shooting memorandum and subsequent investigative report, with as much gusto as he announced the investigation. He could have easily made the announcement prior to the release of the grand jury's findings and calmed the waters throughout the nation. Instead, he chastises police to not use force or to use force judiciously. Duh, that's what law enforcement does.

Even while taunted with expletives, racial epithets, pummeled with rocks and bottles, and facing automatic weapon fire on a nightly basis, the officers and commanders working the Ferguson detail exemplified all that is good with law enforcement and their commitment to serve and protect. One would wonder if Mr. Holder ever spent a moment or two with the officers in Ferguson. Probably not. Didn't want to get his hands dirty. Come on, Mr. Attorney General, really.

AL-JAZEERA INCIDENT

The evening of August 14, 2014 is hot. St. Louis hot. Muggy, you can take a shower, walk out of your house and feel like a wet sponge.

It's hot on West Florissant Avenue in Ferguson, Missouri. The St. Louis suburb propelled onto the international scene. White cop shoots unarmed black teen. The press always fails to add that the black man was shot after he attacked a police officer and attempted to grab his weapon. One can deduce he would have used the weapon to shoot the officer. A black teen, a white police officer—news outlets love to get over involved in this situation.

It's also hot because of all the media on West Florissant Avenue—local, national, and international. The world's hot spot for longer than it should be. Certainly longer than necessary.

Al-Jazeera, one of the fine international news organizations, obligated to stir up racial unrest wherever they may travel.

On this night, a camera crew set up downwind from the protesters/rioters.

Four St. Louis county police detectives proceeded northeast on West Florissant, traveling to a "hotspot" where rioters were getting further out of control. Upon reaching the vicinity of the Al-Jazeera camera crew, a group of people came out from between two buildings and pelted the police car with bricks, bottles, and assorted debris. The windshield cracked, the doors dented.

The detectives stopped and gave chase. To break up the raucous group, several tear gas grenades were tossed. This action dispersed the brick and bottle throwers. The detectives got back into the battered police car and proceeded to the center of activity.

In the process, tear gas wafts to the location of the Al-Jazeera camera

155

crew. Not being equipped with gas masks, the subjects manning the location were overcome with the effects of the tear gas and retreated from their locale.

Several moments later, a tactical team arrives. The officers took down the lights, not in an attempt to harm or damage equipment, but in an effort to deny the rioters a target. The officers guarded the equipment until the gas dissipated and the camera crew returned.

The officers assisted the Al-Jazeera newsies in loading the cameras and associated equipment into the Al-Jazeera van. The cops then helped them relocate to a safer area.

An officer can be heard on a video saying, "You want to go toward Chambers (road), we can help you with that. We don't want you to get hurt."

The officers then afforded safe passage to the crew.

Alas, the 10 p.m. news showed the tactical team arriving, taking down the equipment, and the stern-looking anchor saying the police deliberately threw tear gas at the camera crew and started to destroy the expensive equipment. Just another example of police "trampling" on the constitution's first amendment right to freedom of the press. With his faced scrunched up like somebody just farted, a local reporter says, "I'm Norman Numbnuts, Eyewitless news reporting live from Ferguson, Missouri, where peaceful demonstrators are exercising their right to protest and the racist police threw tear gas at an Al-Jazeera news crew. Blah, blah, blah."

One could wonder what would have happened to all that expensive equipment had someone other than the police not arrived and secured the area until it became possible for the rightful operators to regain control of their broadcast items.

Rather than destroying the expensive filming gear, and disrupting the news process, police officers secured the area. Doing their sworn duty to "Serve and Protect."

"HANDS UP, DON'T SHOOT" BUILT ON A LIE

The words of Jonathan Capehart, a Washington Post columnist, often critical of police actions and activities states that the "Hands up, don't shoot" scenario is built on a lie.

Capehart, in his column said, " ... the unarmed 18-year old also became a potent symbol of the lack of trust between African-Americans and law enforcement—not just in Ferguson, but the entire country. Lord knows there have been plenty of recent examples. And the militarized response to protesters by local police put an exclamation point on demonstrators concerns. But the DOJ report on the actual shooting of Michael Brown shows him to be an inappropriate symbol.

Through exhaustive interviews with witnesses, cross-checking their statements with previous statements to authorities and the media, ballistics, DNA evidence, and results from autopsies, the justice department was able to present a credible and troubling picture of what happened on Canfield Drive.

What the DOJ found made me ill. Wilson knew about the theft of the cigarillos from the convenience store and had a description of the suspects. Brown fought with the officer and tried to take his gun. And the popular "hands-up" storyline, which isn't corroborated by ballistic and DNA evidence or multiple witness statements, was perpetuated by Dorian Johnson. In fact, just about everything said to the media by Johnson, the friend with Brown that day, was not supported by the evidence and other witness statements.

While there are other individuals who stated that Officer Wilson reached out of the SUV and grabbed Brown by the neck, prosecutors could not credit their accounts, because they were inconsistent with physical and forensic evidence.

The forensic evidence consisted of none of Officer Wilson's DNA being found on Brown's shirt. If Officer Wilson did grab Brown by the neck as relayed by Dorian Johnson, his DNA would be on the shirt.

"The DOJ report notes that Johnson made multiple statements to the media immediately following the incident that spawned the popular narrative that Officer Wilson shot Brown execution style as he held his hands up in surrender. In one of those interviews, Johnson told MSNBC that Officer Wilson shot Brown in the back. It was then that Johnson said Brown stopped, turned around with his hands up and said, "I don't have a gun, stop shooting!" And, just like that, "Hands up, don't shoot" became the mantra of a movement. But it was built on a lie.

Capehart further stated, "We must never allow ourselves to march under the banner of a false narrative on behalf of someone who would otherwise offend our sense of right and wrong. And when we discover that we have, we must acknowledge it, admit our error, and keep on marching. That's what I've done here."

Filling in for MSNBC's Chris Matthews, Hardball, Capehart told viewers that he has faced an onslaught of racial attacks since his editorial debunked Ferguson protester's "Hands up, don't shoot" narrative.

Capehart said, "The rage towards anyone who dares to enter that arena and say something that defies conventional wisdom also lurks perpetually. After my piece, "Hands up, don't shoot," was built on a lie, folks used Twitter and Facebook to dismember my personhood. Fellow African American's called me a 'sellout' or a 'house negro.' Others said I did it because I wanted to be liked by white people or that I did it for the money. No, I didn't—I did it because it was the right thing to do. Such taunts won't keep me from speaking my mind."

Well said, sir, well said.

TWO-BIT POLITICIANS

The hue and cry goes up. The cops are "scaring" the protesters by wearing riot gear and by the use of armored vehicles, courtesy of the Department of Defense. Vehicles that in a time not long ago were on the battlefields of Iraq and Afghanistan.

In a total knee-jerk reaction, Missouri Senator Claire McCaskill and Governor Jay, Ah … Um, Nixon proclaim that they will immediately look into the practice of the Department of Defense giving certain equipment to police departments throughout the country.

McCaskill immediately calls for and presides over an inquiry called "The Militarization of Local Police Departments." The hearings held by McCaskill-chaired financial and contracting oversight subcommittee, follows the Democrat's calls for demilitarization in Ferguson, Missouri. "We need to demilitarize this situation—this kind of response by the police has become the problem instead of the solution," McCaskill said while in Ferguson shortly after the shooting death of Mike Brown. Jr. It should be noted that McCaskill never got close to the action and thus did not have the opportunity to hear automatic gunfire from the interior of the crowd of "peaceful protesters." Nor was the brave and virtuous senator able to see the rocks, frozen water bottles, and other assorted missiles bouncing off the helmets and shields of the officers attempting to retain some sort of normalcy to the chaotic situation. Brave, yes, most brave indeed.

Comes, once again, Governor Jay, Ah … Um, Nixon with the "pile-on" mentality that one would expect of a governor who demanded a "Vigorous Prosecution," not a "Vigorous Investigation," into the facts and circumstances surrounding the Michael Brown incident.

Jay, Ah … Um, Nixon made the rounds of the Sunday talk shows. Sticking out his chest, quick to condemn and chastise police. He called the tactics of the St. Louis county police "aggressive" and expressed relief that the justice department is conducting its own investigation into the death of Michael Brown, Jr.

Continuing, "There are times when force is necessary, but we really felt that push at that time was a little aggressive, obviously, and those images were not what we were trying to get to. And in those situations where folks are rolling up in heavily armored vehicles, and individually (one can only guess he means riot gear), it's impossible to have a dialogue."

Governor Ah … Um also criticized the police department's release of a convenience store surveillance video that shows Brown and Dorian Johnson stealing a box of cigars from the Ferguson Market. Old Ah … Um went on to state that the tape release is an attempt to "besmirch a victim" and "to tarnish him. It appeared to, you know, cast aspersions on a young man that was gunned down in the street." What about this word we keep hearing, oh yes, transparency? Or does that only apply to certain aspects of this case?

Nixon also raised doubts about the special prosecutor in charge of the case, St. Louis County Prosecuting Attorney Robert McCullough. (Note to Ah … Um, Bob McCullough IS the prosecuting attorney, NOT a special prosecutor.)

Offering little confidence in the investigative expertise of the St. Louis county police department, Nixon said he is pleased that the justice department is conducting its own parallel inquiry, noting that the FBI is sending 40 investigators. "That's the kind of independent, external, national review, and investigation of this that I think will assist everyone in making sure we get to justice."

Not wanting to let the race aspect of the situation wile away old Ah … Um, said "We all know there's been a long history of challenges in these areas (of Missouri) and our hope is that, with the help of the people here, that we can be an example of getting justice and getting peace and using that to move forward."

Even other cops got in on the snarky comments. Case in point, Chief Mike Koval of the Madison, Wisconsin police department, stated he can "teach a monkey how to shoot a gun. I can't teach him relation skills." According to Koval, that's why his department will continue to recruit diverse officers—not the "rent-a-cops" that he says made lots of mistakes in Ferguson. For the record, all Ferguson police department officers are fully credentialed and are the holders of a Missouri Peace Officer Class A license. Not "rent-a-cops." One could wonder how the chief plans to train his officers if someone jumps through the open window of a police car and attempts to grab the officer's gun. Maybe try to "engage" the thug in a conversation about why he would attempt such a stupid maneuver. All this while, the officer is fighting for his life.

On the flip side comes Sheriff David Clarke, Milwaukee County, Wisconsin. In his no nonsense and straightforward way said:

"I'm not one known to sugar coat things. This pissed me off, I sat up and watched as events unfolded in Ferguson, Missouri. It's an unfortunate situation obviously. Anytime a law enforcement officer uses deadly force that takes a life, it deserves a thorough, transparent vetting and investigation, we all agree with that. But then, some groups began to converge on the small town of Ferguson, Missouri, like vultures on a roadside carcass. Groups like the New Black Panther Party. People like Al Sharpton. To come and exploit that situation and instead of coming into help and restore calm, poured gas on a fire with some of their inflammatory and irresponsible rhetoric. I sat up there and listened to Governor (Ah … Um) Nixon and I sat up and listened to Claire McCaskill the senator and then I sat up there and listened to Eric Holder throw law enforcement officers under the bus for political expediency. These are the same individuals at election time who come around wanting support from law enforcement organizations—I expect that from Governor Nixon. I expected that from Senator McCaskill—those are nothing but two-bit politicians, they do that sort of thing, that's what politicians do. You know that … but I did not expect that from Eric Holder, who calls himself a law enforcement officer."

Events in Ferguson played out. The investigations into the death of Michael Brown, Jr. by the justice department and the St. Louis county police both found Police Officer Darren Wilson, in fact, justified in his use of deadly force that hot, muggy August day.

The St. Louis county prosecuting attorney, Bob McCullough, convened a grand jury. After several months of testimony and review of the physical and scientific evidence, the grand jury did not indict Officer Wilson.

Shortly after the grand jury decision, the justice department revealed that there would be no charges against Officer Wilson. The justice department report stated that "hands up, don't shoot" was and is a totally false premise. Their investigation concluded that Brown attacked Officer Wilson as he sat in his marked police SUV and attempted to gain control of his weapon. In essence, the use of deadly force, in this instance, is justified.

In an unusual move, the St. Louis County prosecuting attorney went before a circuit judge and requested that ALL testimony and evidence in the grand jury proceedings be released. They were, and for those that are scratching their collective heads about transparency, take a look at the voluminous and extensive transcripts of the grand jury.

The grand jury review, conducted in a professional and skilled manner could find no evidence to charge Officer Wilson. But then, Officer Wilson is not a ham sandwich.

The hope that Governor Ah ... Um, Nixon would wind up as the vice-presidential candidate on a Hillary ticket crashed and burned.

Senator McCaskill, who stated on a number of occasions that she would be honored to serve as the governor of the Great State of Missouri has, sadly, withdrawn from any attempt to attain that office.

Quick note to two-bit politicians: police officers, their families, and their sphere of influence vote a hell of a lot more than rioters. They also vote for those that support them. Individuals that do not jump to premature conclusions and blame police for the unlawful actions of others ... just a note. Is there room under that bus for a few two-bit politicians? Hope so.

YOU KNEW IT WAS GOING
TO HAPPEN

It's a little after midnight. Police officers from several jurisdictions in St. Louis County manned a line in front of the Ferguson police department. Eight months of demonstrations and riots befell the city of Ferguson.

The evening of March 11, 2015, "peaceful demonstrators" strode up and down West Florissant Avenue. This evening Ferguson police chief Tom Jackson announced he would retire. A group of coalitions that sprung up after the shooting of Michael Brown with righteous sounding names demanded the resignation of the chief. Citing unnamed sources and drawing from the Shit Disturbers Handbook, the self-appointed leaders claimed that Chief Jackson presided over a racist and corrupt police department. Statements made with no factual basis.

One would think those involved in the marching and mayhem would be pleased to have hounded the chief out of his position. But no, the crowd of around one-hundred and fifty became more enraged. One can only opine why. Fights broke out in the gathering. Angry words exchanged. This time between the protesters, not directed at the police. Tension filled the air. Nerves on edge. Protesters hurling racial slurs at each other. Fists flying. Police waded into the fray, separated the groups and even convinced some of those in attendance to leave the area. Tomorrow is another day, you can come back and continue to protest under better conditions. Some protesters even took the advice and departed the area. Some, not all.

Jeffrey Williams, a 20-year-old jerk involved in earlier fist fights, stuck around making an ass of himself. Williams finally retreated to the top of a hill approximately 125 yards from the line of police officers standing in front of the Ferguson police department. Shortly after midnight, Williams wrapped his grubby hands around the handle of a .40 caliber handgun and fired a number of shots in the general direction of the Ferguson police department.

One of the bullets struck a Webster Groves police officer in the face. The officer had the face shield of his riot helmet down. The round struck the helmet shield and traveled into his face directly below his left eye. The slug traveled through flesh and bone coming to rest near his ear. The face shield slowed the bullets velocity significantly. Had he not been wearing his helmet the wad of lead may have traveled further with the potential of causing traumatic brain injury. Remember when the protester wanted the police not to wear helmets because it scared and intimidated them?

One of the other rounds struck a St. Louis county police officer in the shoulder. The round traveled through his body coming to a stop near his back.

Several officers saw the muzzle flashes and directed their attention toward the source of the gunshots.

An intense and focused investigation followed the shooting. TV cameras rolled. Police asked for help from anyone who may have any information. Detectives conducted interviews trying to shake some information out of a reluctant constituency.

A police informant had knowledge of the offense and contacted St. Louis county detectives and identified the shooter as Mr. Williams. Through the investigative process, arrest and search warrants were obtained and served on Williams' place of abode. Detectives recovered the .40 caliber pistol and took the suspect into custody without incident.

After weaving a number of tales, detectives determined that Williams fired the weapon that struck the two officers. Williams told investigators that he was not shooting at the police officers. He merely shot with the intent to strike those with whom he had a previous altercation while "peacefully protesting."

St. Louis county prosecuting attorney, Bob McCulloch, in a statement after the arrest of the suspect stated that the shell casings found at the site where the weapon fired matched up with the handgun recovered during the execution of a search warrant at Williams' residence. McCulloch thanked the community for coming forward with information that lead to the arrest of Williams. Additionally, McCulloch said that Williams claimed he was not shooting at police, but rather shooting at someone else—a story viewed with a somewhat skeptical eye. The end result was that two cops were shot while standing in front of the Ferguson police department.

St Louis County Police Chief Jon Belmar said, "We could have buried two police officers."

Williams charged with assault in the first degree, firing a weapon from a vehicle, and armed criminal action. Bond set at $300,000, cash only.

Williams, while a guest of the St. Louis county justice center, had a number of telephone conversations with his pregnant girlfriend. All inmates are advised that their phone conversations are monitored and recorded and can be used as evidence against them. The warning also contained the fact that these conversations are matters of public record. Despite the warning, Williams spoke freely with his girlfriend.

In one conversation, Williams said he was harassed by a group of people outside the Ferguson police station. "Nobody aiming at no police, I ran up the hill and he (unidentified person) shot at the car … I shot back," he said.

In another recorded conversation, he expressed dismay at the possibility of a lengthy prison sentence saying, "Even though I was in the wrong though, I should have just went the other way, oh man, now I'm lookin' at ten years."

Williams' attorney said he told him he never fired during the protest. He also criticized the justice center for releasing audio that provides evidence against Williams. The tapes, released after a freedom of information request, filed on behalf of a local news outlet. Remember that bit about "public records"?

Williams' attorney criticized the justice center for releasing the audio that provides potential evidence against Williams. He said, "My client maintained to me that he never fired a gun that night, so until I'm able to see the evidence that I can distinctly talk to him about, I have to maintain my commitment to the statements that he has made to me."

Everyone exposed to our criminal justice system is entitled to remain silent. Some lack the ability to do so.

DEPARTMENT OF JUSTICE MEMORANDUM

RE: Shooting of Michael Brown, Jr.

The following are excerpts from the United States Department of Justice memorandum, dated March 4, 2015 stating the justice department could find no evidence in support of a civil right action against former Ferguson Police Officer Darren Wilson.

"Although there are several individuals who have stated that Brown held his hands up in an unambiguous sign of surrender prior to Officer Wilson shooting him dead, their accounts do not support a prosecution of Officer Wilson. As detailed throughout this report, some of those accounts are materially inconsistent with the physical and forensic evidence; some of those accounts are materially inconsistent with the witness' own prior statements with no explanation, creditable or otherwise, as to why those accounts changed over time. (A valid reason the testimony and accounts changed is that autopsy results and forensic evidence showed Brown's DNA on the officers clothing, weapon and the interior of the police unit.) Certain other witnesses who originally stated Brown had his hands up in surrender recanted their original accounts, admitting that they did not witness the shooting or parts of it, despite what they initially reported either to law enforcement, federal or local, or to the media.

While credible witnesses gave varying accounts of exactly what Brown was doing with his hands as he moved toward Wilson—for example, balling them, holding them out or pulling up his pants—and varying accounts of how he was moving—such as "charging," moving in "slow motion," or "running"—they all establish that Brown was moving toward Wilson when Wilson shot him. Although some witnesses state that Brown held his hands up at shoulder level with his palms facing outward for a brief moment, these same witnesses describe Brown then dropping his hands and "charging" at Officer Wilson.

Initial Law Enforcement Investigation

Officer Wilson shot Brown at about 12:02 p.m. on August 9, 2014. Within minutes, FPD officers responded to the scene, as they were already en route from Wilson's initial radio call for assistance. Also within minutes, residents began pouring onto the street. At 12:08 p.m., FPD officers requested assistance from nearby SLCPD precincts. By 12:14 p.m., some members of the growing crowd became increasingly hostile in response to chants of "[We] need to kill these motherfuckers," referring to the police officers at the scene. At around the same time, a FPD sergeant informed the FPD chief that there had been a fatal officer-involved shooting. At about 12:23 p.m., the FPD chief contacted the SLCPD chief and turned over the homicide investigation to the SLCPD. Within twenty minutes of Brown's death, paramedics covered Brown's body with several white sheets.

The SLCPD division of criminal investigation homicide unit was notified at 12:43 p.m. and advised to conduct the homicide investigation. Homicide units arrived at the scene at approximately 1:30 p.m. They were involved in a hostage situation at the opposite end of St. Louis county and arrived approximately 37 minutes after being notified.

Between about 12:45 p.m. and 1:17 p.m., SLCPD reported gunfire in the area, putting both civilians and officers in danger. As a result, canine officers and additional patrol officers responded to assist with crowd control. SLCPD expanded the perimeter of the crime scene to move the crowd away from Brown's body in an effort to preserve the crime scene for processing.

Upon arrival of St. Louis county crime scene investigation detectives, orange privacy screens were placed around the body of Michael Brown, Jr. Homicide detectives then alerted the St. Louis county medical examiner to respond to the scene. To further protect the integrity of the crime scene and in accordance with common practice, SLCPD personnel did not permit family members and concerned neighbors into the crime scene. According to SLCPD detectives, they have one opportunity to investigate thoroughly a crime scene before it is forever changed upon the removal of the decedent's body. Processing a homicide scene with the decedent's body present allows detectives, for example, to measure distances accurately, precisely document body position, and note injury and other markings relative to other aspects of the crime scene that photographs may not capture.

In this case, crime scene detectives had to stop processing the scene as a result of two more reports of what sounded like automatic weapons gunfire in the area at 1:55 p.m. and 2:11 p.m., as well as some individuals in the crowd encroaching on the crime scene and chanting "Kill the police," as documented in cell phone video. At each of those times, having exhausted their existing resources SLCPD personnel called emergency codes for additional patrol officers throughout St. Louis county in increments of twenty-five. Livery drivers sent to transport Brown's body upon completion of processing arrived at 2:20 p.m. Their customary practice is to wait on scene until the body is ready for transport. However, an SLCPD sergeant briefly stopped them from getting out of their vehicle until the gunfire abated and it was safe for them to do so. Witnesses and detectives described the scene as volatile causing concern for both their personal safety and the integrity of the crime scene. The initial investigation at the scene completed at approximately 4:00 p.m., at which time Brown's body was transported to the office of the medical examiner.

Legal Summary

The evidence does not establish that the shots fired by Officer Wilson were objectively unreasonable under federal law. The physical evidence established Wilson shot Brown once in the hand at close range, while Wilson sat in the police SUV, struggling with Brown for control of Wilson's gun. Wilson then shot Brown several more times from a distance of at least two feet after Brown ran away from Wilson and then turned around and faced him. There are no witness accounts that federal prosecutors, and likewise, a jury, would credit to support a conclusion that Wilson fired at Brown from behind. Medical examiner reports are in agreement that the entry wounds to Brown's right arm, which indicate neither bullet trajectory nor the direction in which Brown was moving when he was struck. Medical examiner reports are in agreement that the entry wounds from the latter were to the front of Brown's body, establishing that Brown was facing Wilson when these shots were fired. This includes the fatal shot to the top of Brown's head. The physical evidence also establishes that Brown moved forward toward Wilson after he turned around to face him. The physical evidence is corroborated by multiple eyewitnesses.

Applying the well-established controlling legal authority, including binding precedent from the United States supreme court and the eighth circuit court of appeals, the evidence does not establish that it was unreasonable for Officer Wilson to perceive Brown as a threat, while Brown was punching and grabbing him in the SUV and attempting to take his gun. Thereafter, when Brown started to flee, Officer Wilson was aware that Brown attempted to take his gun and suspected that Brown might have been part of a theft a few minutes before. Under the law, it was not unreasonable for Officer Wilson to perceive that Brown posed a threat of serious physical harm, either to him or others. When Brown turned around and moved toward Officer Wilson, the applicable law and evidence do not support finding that Officer Wilson was not unreasonable in his fear that Brown would once again attempt to harm him and gain control of his gun. There are no credible witness accounts that state that Brown was clearly attempting to surrender when Officer Wilson shot him. As detailed throughout this report, those witnesses who say so have given accounts that could not be relied upon in a prosecution because they were irreconcilable with the physical evidence, inconsistent with the credible accounts of other eyewitnesses, inconsistent with the witnesses own prior statements, or in some instances, because the witnesses have acknowledged that their initial accounts were untrue.

DNA Analysis

The SLCPD crime laboratory conducted DNA analysis taken from Officer Wilson, Brown, Officer Wilson's gun, and the crime scene. Brown's DNA was found at four significant locations: on Officer Wilson's gun; on the roadway further away from where he died; on the SUV driver's side door and inside the driver's cabin area of the SUV; and on Officer Wilson's clothes. A DNA mixture from which Officer Wilson's DNA could not be extracted was found on Brown's left palm.

DNA analysis of Brown's clothes, right hand, fingernails, and clothes excluded Wilson as a possible contributor. (This debunks Dorian Johnson's testimony before the St. Louis county grand jury that Brown and Officer Wilson were in a tug-of-war with Brown's shirt. Additionally, Johnson's initial story that Officer Wilson reached out of the police SUV and grabbed Brown's shirt is not true.)

Officer Wilson's Medical Records

Paramedics examined Officer Wilson when he returned to the FPD after the shooting, and recommended that he go to the hospital for follow-up treatment. Officer Wilson sought medical treatment at Christian Northwest Hospital within two hours of the shooting. To make a medical determination, the nurse practitioner questioned Officer Wilson about what happened. Officer Wilson stated that he was twice punched in the jaw. The nurse practitioner noted acute or fresh pink scratch marks on the back of Officer Wilson's neck as well as swelling to his jaw. Wilson sustained contusions of the jaw area, but did not break any other bones. According to the nurse practitioner, Officer Wilson's injuries were consistent with his description of what transpired.

Officer Wilson submitted to a drug and alcohol screen. His blood alcohol content was 0.00% and tested negative for any drugs.

Brown's Toxicology

A toxicologist with the St. Louis University toxicology laboratory and the chief of the division of forensic toxicology at the armed forces medical examiner's section each conducted blood and urine screens on samples collected from Brown's body. Brown tested positive for the presence of canabinoids, THC, the hallucinogenic substances associated with marijuana use. The St. Louis University toxicology laboratory found 12 nanograms per milliliter of the active ingredient. The armed forces medical examiner's section found 11 nanograms per milliliter of the active ingredient.

According to both laboratories, these levels of the marijuana active ingredient are consistent with Brown having ingested THC within hours before his death. This concentration of THC would have rendered Brown impaired at the time of his death. As a general matter, this level of impairment can alter one's perception of time and space, but the extent to which this was true in Brown's case cannot be determined. (Toxicology report attached.)

Legal Analysis

The evidence is insufficient to establish probable cause or to prove beyond a reasonable doubt a violation of the applicable federal statute occurred and would not likely to survive a defense motion for acquittal at trial pursuant to Federal Rule of Criminal Procedure. This is true for all six to eight shots that struck brown. Witness accounts suggesting that Brown was standing still with his hands raised in an unambiguous signal of surrender when Officer Wilson shot Brown are inconsistent with the physical evidence, are otherwise not credible because of internal inconsistencies, or are not credible because of inconsistencies with other credible evidence. In contrast, Officer Wilson's account of Brown's actions, if true, would establish that the shootings were not objectively unreasonable under the relevant constitutional standards governing an officer's use of deadly force. Multiple credible witnesses corroborate virtually every material aspect of Wilson's account and are consistent with the physical evidence. Even if the evidence established that Officer Wilson's actions were unreasonable, the government would also have to prove that Officer Wilson acted willfully, that is, that he acted with a specific intent to violate the law. As discussed previously, Officer Wilson's stated intent for shooting Brown was in response to a deadly threat. Therefore, the only possible basis for prosecuting Officer Wilson under section 242 would be if the government could prove that his account is not true—that is, that Brown never punched and grabbed Officer Wilson at the SUV, never struggled with Officer Wilson over the gun, and thereafter clearly surrendered in a way that no reasonable officer could have failed to perceive. Not only do eyewitness and physical evidence corroborate Officer Wilson's account, but no credible evidence exists to disprove Officer Wilson's perception that Brown posed a threat to him as he advanced toward him. Accordingly, seeking his indictment is not permitted by the Department of Justice policy or the governing law.

No one disputes that Officer Wilson, who was on duty and working as a police officer for the FPD, acted under color of law when he shot Brown or that the shots resulted in Brown's death. Determining if criminal prosecution is appropriate rests on whether sufficient evidence exists to establish that any of the shots fired by Officer Wilson were unreasonable given the facts known to Officer Wilson at the time. If so, whether Officer Wilson fired the shots with the requisite "willful" criminal intent, which, in this case, would require proof that he shot Brown under conditions that no reasonable officer could have perceived as a threat.

St. Louis University Toxicology Laboratory Report
6059 N. Hanley Road, Berkeley, Missouri 63134

Name: BROWN, MICHAEL   Tox # 2014-5156
  Age: 18 years   Race: Black   Sex: Male

Requesting Agency: ST. LOUIS COUNTY MEDICAL EXAMINER
  (Agency's Case No.: 14-5143)

===
Blood:

  Alcohol:
    Ethanol: _____ Negative
    Acetone: _____ Negative
    Isopropanol: _____ Negative
    Methanol: _____ Negative

  Blood Drug Screen:
    Amphetamines: _____ Negative
    Antidepressants: _____ Negative
    Barbiturates: _____ Negative
    Benzodiazepines: _____ Negative
    CANNABINOIDS: _____ POSITIVE
    Cocaine/Metabolites: _____ Negative
    Lidocaine: _____ Negative
    Methadone: _____ Negative
    Non-Opiate Narcotic Analgesic: _____ Negative
    Opiates: _____ Negative
    Phencyclidine: _____ Negative
    Phenothiazines: _____ Negative
    Propoxyphene: _____ Negative
    Acetaminophen: _____ Negative
    Salicylates: _____ Negative
    Oxycodone: _____ Negative
    Fentanyl: _____ Negative
    Oxymorphone: _____ Negative

  Cannabinoid Quantitation:
    DELTA-9-THC: _____ 12 NANOGRAMS/ML
    11-HYDROXY-THC: _____ Negative
    11-NOR-DELTA-9-THC-COOH: _____ 45 NANOGRAMS/ML

Urine:

  Cannabinoid Quantitation:
    DELTA-9-THC: _____ Negative
    11-HYDROXY-THC: _____ GREATER THAN 25 NANOGRAMS/ML
    11-NOR-DELTA-9-THC-COOH: _____ GREATER THAN 150 NANOGRAMS/ML

===

Requested by: DR   Date: 08/10/14

Received in Lab: Date/Time: 08/11/14//05:45 AM

Report by: DR.   Date/Time: 08/15/2014//08:50 AM

St. Louis University Toxicology Laboratory Report
6059 N. Hanley Road, Berkeley, Missouri 63134

Name: BROWN, MICHAEL   Tox # 2014-5156
   Age: 18 years   Race: Black   Sex: Male

Comments: Delta-9-THC detection in the blood defines impairment.

==

Requested by: DR   Date: 08/10/14

Received in Lab: Date/Time: 08/11/14//05:45 AM

Report by: Date/Time: 08/15/2014//08:50 AM

Were the government to prosecute Officer Wilson, the court would instruct the jury using previous decisions as a foundation. Given the circumstances and evidence in this matter, jurors would likely conclude that Officer Wilson had reason to be concerned that Brown was a threat to him, as he continued to advance.

In addition, even assuming that Officer Wilson definitively knew that Brown was not armed, he was aware that Brown had already assaulted him once and attempted to gain control of his gun. Officer Wilson could thus present evidence that he reasonably feared that, if left unimpaired, Brown would again assault and attempt to overpower him, and attempt to retake his gun. Under the law, Officer Wilson has a strong argument that he was justified in firing his weapon at Brown as he continued to advance toward him and refused commands to stop. The law does not require Officer Wilson to wait until Brown was close enough to assault him physically. With hindsight, even if Officer Wilson could have done something other than shoot Brown, the fourth amendment does not second-guess a law enforcement officer's decision on how to respond to an advancing threat.

Because Officer Wilson did not act with the requisite criminal intent, no one can prove beyond a reasonable doubt to a jury that Officer Wilson violated any federal law when he fired his weapon at Brown.

Conclusion

For the previous reasons set forth, this matter lacks prosecutive merit and should be closed.

DEPARTMENT OF JUSTICE FERGUSON REPORT

On March 4, 2015, the Civil Rights Division of the US Department of Justice released a report on an in-depth investigation of the Ferguson police department. Also released on March 4, 2015 is the report of the criminal investigation into the shooting of Michael Brown by Ferguson police officer Darren Wilson. The report on the shooting of Michael Brown revealed that the police officer, while being attacked by Michael Brown, complied with all federal and state laws. The justice department and the St. Louis county grand jury did not charge the officer.

The report on the Ferguson police department found a number of faults and attempted to articulate them in this report. The first page of the report contains the following statement:

We thank the city officials and the rank and file who have cooperated in this investigation and provided us with insights into the operation of the police department, including the municipal court. Notwithstanding our findings about Ferguson's approach to law enforcement and the policing culture creates, we found many Ferguson police officers and other city employees to be dedicated public servants striving each day to perform their duties lawfully and with respect for all members of the Ferguson community. The importance of their often-selfless work cannot be overstated.

From this point, the report does not put the Ferguson police department in a flattering light. On page 4, the report states:

Ferguson's law-enforcement practices overwhelmingly impact African-Americans. Data collected by the Ferguson police department from 2012 to 2014 shows that African-Americans account for 85 percent of vehicle stops, 80 percent of citations, and 93 percent of arrests made by FPD officers, despite comprising only 67 percent of Ferguson's population.

In a 2011 Bureau of Justice Statistics Police, Public Contact Survey, the data indicates that African-Americans are 31 percent more likely to be pulled over than white drivers. The survey also reveals that men are 42 percent more likely than women to be pulled over for traffic violations. Are cops throughout the country biased against males?

A 2006 National Highway Traffic Safety Administration study found black drivers killed in accidents have the highest rate of past convictions for speeding and other moving violations. This figure would suggest there are a lot of unsafe black drivers, not racism.

The Justice Department report continues:

African-Americans are at least 50 percent more likely to have their cases lead to an arrest warrant. This accounted for 92 percent of cases in which an arrest warrant was issued by the Ferguson municipal court in 2013. This indicates racism.

The report does not look at or explain how many offenders made court appearances on the scheduled date or paid their fine. Non-appearance in court is a big factor in issuing a warrant. The justice department went through the files, however, failed to address the subject of court appearances and fine payment.

In the event you think this is unique to Ferguson, the next time you are issued a traffic ticket, try not making an appearance in court and see what happens. Chances are a warrant will be issued for your arrest. It doesn't make any difference where your ticket originates. Anecdotal evidence by the justice department offers to bring home this complaint:

That blacks are the "victim" of an oppressive police department and court system.

Anecdotal, according to the Oxford American Dictionary is, "NOT NECESSARILY TRUE, BECAUSE BASED ON SOMEONE'S PERSONAL ACCOUNT OF AN EVENT, RATHER THAN ON FACTS."

Then there's the tale of an oppressive police department and overreaching court system in Washington DC, a city with a black mayor and predominately black city council.

Megan Johnson, a black DC woman, recently failed to pay ten parking tickets within the allotted 30 days. The city doubled the fine from $500 to $1,000, booted, towed, and sold her car. In addition, she received a $700 charge for storing her car.

The city sold her car for $500 and won't even credit that amount to what she owes. DC is now attaching her tax refunds. Is this anecdotal evidence of racism? Mr. Attorney General, maybe you and your band of roving statisticians need to look in your own back yard.

Under Municipal Court Practices, the report states:

Ferguson has allowed its focus on revenue generation to fundamentally compromise the mission of Ferguson's municipal court. The municipal court does not act as a neutral arbiter of the law or check on unlawful police conduct. Instead, the court primarily uses its judicial authority as the means to compel payment of fines and fees that advance the city's financial interests.

Missouri law allows a municipality to derive no more than 30 percent of its total revenue from court fines and fees. The Ferguson portion of the courts addition to the city of Ferguson's general revenue is somewhere near 15 percent—well within the constraints of the law.

To change this, the governor, Jay, ah ... Um, Nixon, could and probably should, attend to the formation and issuance of a new law that further restricts using municipal courts as a fund generator for a city's revenue.

Some unconstitutional practices were institutionalized in a process best described as a 'legitimacy-through-official-sounding' jargon. Consider the Wanted designation ...

FPD and other law enforcement agencies in St. Louis county use a system of Wanted or Stop Orders as a substitute for seeking judicial approval for an arrest warrant. When an officer believes a person has committed a crime, but are not immediately able to locate that person, they can enter a Wanted into the statewide law enforcement database, indicating to all other law enforcement agencies that the person should be arrested if located. While wanted are supposed to be based on probable cause, they operate as an end-run around the judicial system. Instead of swearing out a warrant and seeking judicial authorization from neutral and detached magistrate, officers make probable-cause determination themselves and circumvent the courts.

If officers enter Wanted into the system on less than probable cause, the subsequent arrest would violate the fourth amendment. Our interviews with command staff and officers indicate that officers do not clearly understand the legal authority necessary to issue a Wanted. For example, one veteran officer gave the example of investigating a car theft. Upon identifying the suspect, he would put that suspect into the system as Wanted, "because we do not have probable cause that he stole the vehicle." Reflecting the muddled analysis officers may employ when deciding to issue a Wanted, this officer concluded, "You have to have reasonable suspicion and some probable cause to put out a Wanted.

In December 2014, a Ferguson detective investigating a shooting emailed a county prosecutor to see if a warrant for a suspect could be obtained. The prosecutor responded stating that although "chances are" the crime was committed by the suspect, "we just don't have enough for a warrant right now.

The detective responded that he would enter a Wanted. There is evidence that the use of Wanted has resulted in numerous unconstitutional arrests in Ferguson.

A Wanted arrest order is primarily used by detectives in furtherance of an active investigation, based on reasonable cause—not probable cause. To close a case, a detective will be required to interview the suspect. At the conclusion of the suspect interview, the investigator will finalize the report and submit the finished product to the prosecuting attorney. At this juncture, the decision to issue an arrest warrant is made based upon the facts and circumstances of the case.

A Wanted is issued when the officer cannot immediately locate a suspect. Once the subject is taken into custody and interviewed, the individual is either released or charged with an arrest warrant. It's really pretty simple. In actuality, an active detective will only issue a Wanted between 10 to 20 times during a career. This hardly qualifies as " ... numerous unconstitutional arrests in Ferguson.

The use of a Wanted is well within the law and would not need to be used, if the focus of an investigation would be available to the investigator to complete the investigation underway. Many times a violator will flee the area or dodge attempts to locate the suspect. When observing the Wanted system in its totality, it is reasonable to see that this is an investigative tool. It is not used, as the justice department would have everyone believe, as a haphazard way to irritate and harass the public. NOT TRUE, MR. HOLDER.

According to the Missouri Law Review, published by the University of Missouri Law School:

... Most courts that have considered the question in recent years have held that the Fourth Amendment does not prohibit warrantless arrests ... In United States v. Watson, the Supreme Court upheld a warrantless, public felony arrest made pursuant to a federal law authorizing "arrests without warrant for felonies," if there are "reasonable" grounds to believe that the person to be arrested has committed or is committing such a felony. The majority took the position that the court's prior cases construing the Fourth Amendment reflected "the ancient common-law rule that a peace officer was permitted to arrest without a warrant for a misdemeanor or felony committed in his presence as well as a felony not committed in his presence, if there was reasonable ground for making the arrest." In addition, the majority observed that the rule "authorizing felony arrests on probable cause, but without a warrant, has survived substantially intact ... In almost all of the states," was the rule recommended by the American Law Institute, and "is the rule Congress has long directed its principle law enforcement officers to follow."

The court noted the advantages of arrest warrants, but specifically declined to transform its preference for such warrants "into a constitutional rule when the judgment of the nation and congress has for so long been to authorize warrantless public arrests on probable cause, rather than to encumber criminal prosecutions with endless litigation with respect to the existence of exigent circumstances."

As a practical matter, a Wanted is most often used by detectives and is used rather sparingly in furtherance of a felony investigation. The Department of Justice report stating that "FPD and other law enforcement agencies in St. Louis County use a system of Wanted or Stop Orders as a substitute for seeking judicial approval for an arrest warrant ... " This is a total falsehood and sloppy investigation by the justice department. If the people conducting this witch-hunt would take the time to fully and thoroughly look into the court cases that support this activity, perhaps a different conclusion would have been drawn. Then again, maybe not.

On the other hand, if the Department of Justice came to the city of Ferguson with an established agenda, the outcome would be the one drawn by the DOJ.

Continuing, the Department of Justice report states:

At times, the constitutional violations are more blatant. An African-American man recounted to us an experience he had while sitting at a bus stop near Canfield Drive. According to the man, an FPD patrol car abruptly pulled up in front of him. The officer inside, a patrol lieutenant, rolled down his window and addressed the man:

Lieutenant: Get over here.

Bus patron: Me?

Lieutenant: Get the f*** over here. Yeah you.

Bus Patron: Why? What did I do?

Lieutenant: Give me your ID

Bus Patron: Why?

Lieutenant: Stop being a smart ass and give me your ID.

The lieutenant ran the man's name for warrants. Finding none, he returned the ID and said, "Get the hell out of my face." These allegations are consistent with other, independent allegations of misconduct that we heard ... and reflect the routinely disrespectful treatment many African-Americans say they have come to expect from Ferguson police. That a lieutenant with supervisory responsibilities allegedly engaged in this conduct is further cause for concern ...

Is this anecdotal evidence? If so, the DOJ should state. Not based on facts, merely a possible non-factual story, told by a person who wants to get in on the party and say things that may or may not be true.

Let's take a look at this "alleged" misconduct. First and foremost, it is most unusual for a lieutenant watch commander to engage in any street-related activities, such as pedestrian and car stops.

Secondly, this is a random selection of the population. The methodology used is not spelled out except to say, "An African-American man recounted to us ... " This brings up the question of, how did this individual come to the attention of the investigators? Did the subject of the activity just drop into the police station and say he wanted to speak with the DOJ investigators? Was this person randomly selected by the DOJ investigators and then told a tall tale? If that is the case, it certainly would not be the first time a person lied to DOJ personnel. You may recall the false and deceiving testimony given to the St. Louis county grand jury as contained in Volume XVI on October 27, 2014. One person in particular stands out when he testified …

Q. Okay, Now when you initially talked to the FBI, and we've listened to your statements … there is information in there that the officer was standing over him while he laid on the ground and finished him off?

A. You know, I said that out of an assumption based on me being where I'm from and that can be the only assumption that I have.

Q. All right. The first time you talked to the FBI, which was a week after this happened, you told them a story that was a bunch of lies, isn't that right?

A. A bunch of lies?

Q. Well, you told them that you saw the officer stand over Michael Brown and empty his clip into the body and finish him off, didn't you say that?

A. Well, you know, I did say that …

Perhaps the person that allegedly became the subject of the verbal assault by the Ferguson police lieutenant told lies and untruths about the Ferguson officer. One could question if the authors of the report on the misdeeds of the FPD made even a feeble attempt to verify that the activity, as alleged, really did occur. I would like to think that those that are accusing the FPD of sloppy investigations and police activities would take the time and effort to check the tale as related by the aggrieved subject.

The report on the FPD, reviewed at the highest level of the justice department. Someone should have questioned the final report and content that a basic investigation could have clarified.

The Department of Justice report continues:

We have discovered evidence of racial bias in emails sent by Ferguson officials, all of whom are current employees, almost without exception through their official city of Ferguson e-mail accounts, and apparently sent during work hours. These email exchanges involved several police and court supervisors and commanders.

The following emails are illustrative:

- A November 2008 email stated that President Obama would not be president long, because "what black man holds a steady job for four years."
- An April 2011 email depicted President Obama as a chimpanzee
- A May 2011 email stated: "An African-American woman in New Orleans was admitted into a hospital for the termination of a pregnancy. Two weeks later, she received a check for $5,000. She phoned the hospital to ask who it was from. The hospital said, 'Crime Stoppers.' "

The report goes on to identify additional emails by the city of Ferguson upper management, in addition to police commanders. Grow up, boys and girls, this is not the type of information to be passed about, especially using the city's time and resources.

Perhaps an overstaffing issue exists, if the city's employees are using valuable work time to exchange these juvenile and unacceptable messages.

At this writing, those responsible for these vicious and uncalled for emails have either retired or been terminated by city government, as they should be. This can be addressed by ensuring that the city's communication system is used for the conduct of city business only. Any deviation from this rule could and probably will result in the loss of the offender's position, including loss of pay and benefits.

The portion of the DOJ report addressing Community Policing states:

Ferguson's community policing efforts appear to have been somewhat modest, but have dwindled to almost nothing in recent years. FPD has no community policing or community engagement plan. FPD currently designates a single officer as the "Community Resource Officer." This officer attends community meetings, serves as FPD's public relations liaison, and is charged with collecting crime data. No other officers play any substantive role in community policing efforts. Officers we spoke with were fairly consistent in their acknowledgment of this, and of the fact that this move away from community policing has been due, at least in part, to an increased focus on code enforcement and revenue generation in recent years.

As discussed previously, our investigation found that FPD redeployed officers to a 12-hour shift, in part for revenue reasons. There is some evidence that community policing is more difficult to carry out when patrol officers are on a 12-hour shift, and this appears to be the case in Ferguson. While many officers support the 12-hour shift, several have told us that these shifts have undermined community policing efforts. One officer said that, "FPD used to have a strong community policing ethic—then we went to a 12-hour day." Another officer told us that the 12-hour schedule, combined with a lack of any attempt to have officers remain within their assigned area, has resulted in a lack of any geographical familiarity by FPD officers. The same officer told us that it is viewed as more positive to write tickets than to "talk with your businesses.

If this is the case, it falls to first-line supervision to ensure that officers are involved in the community. It's up to the first-line supervisor, usually sergeants, to ensure cars are in the assigned beat; that the officers are getting out of the cars, walking housing and business areas, and attending community and church meetings; and talking with business owners and residents to get their input on what concerns they may have. A school resource officer is often a good deterrent to criminal activity. They can, and many times are a role model and mentor to kids "on the edge." At-risk youths can easily be identified. If someone gets between them and the streets before it is too late, a juvenile about to lapse into the gang life can be redirected. Sports and school extracurricular activities are excellent avenues to redirect the child's focus.

The command/staff of the Ferguson police department are responsible for the setting of policy, such as officers must stay in their assigned area unless otherwise directed by radio dispatch or other such necessities for leaving their assigned area. Additionally, policy matters directing community policing activities are made by upper levels of the department. Examples of this are that officers are required to visit each business to update the business information every several months and they are required to get out of their cars and walk a period of time on each shift.

First-line supervision is responsible to see that the policy, as determined by upper management of the department, is followed. All officers stay within their assigned area, unless the need to exchange information or assistance is required. It is often a good idea to have two officers walk a densely populated housing location.

Once again, I question the methodology of this "study." Did any of the writers or any member of the unit doing this study take the time to ride a full shift? Not once, but a number of times. They may have had the opportunity to see the officers interact with members of the public. The DOJ investigators would see the activities involved professional interaction. They would also see officers dealing with street-level offenders, one would like to say in a professional manner. To get a full and objective idea of the issues an officer deals with on a daily or nightly basis, the DOJ team member should ride with the officers for an extended time. I'm going to go out on a limb and say that this did not occur. Guess those folks need their rest … and bad guys are out there.

Concerning the lack of a diverse police department, the report states:

While it does not appear that a lack of racial diversity among officers decreases the trust of African-Americans in a police department, this observation must be qualified.

Increasing a police department's racial diversity does not necessarily increase community trust or improve officer conduct, but there appear to be many causes for this. One important reason is that African-Americans can abuse and violate the rights of African-American civilians, just as white officers can and some African-American officers who have behaved abusively can undermine community trust just as white officers can. Our investigation indicates that in Ferguson, individual officer behavior is largely driven by a police culture and is infected by race bias. While increased vertical and horizontal diversity, racial or otherwise, likely is necessary to change this culture, it probably cannot do so on its own.

What a bunch of gibberish. The Ferguson police department should have more black officers. Although a black man or woman considering a law enforcement career who viewed the black officers being taunted, cursed, and harangued with racial epithets while serving during the "peaceful protests," would or at least should give second thoughts to the pursuit of a law enforcement career. Not to mention the evening display of gunfire and the subsequent shooting of two police officers, which might induce this person probably to think twice about a law enforcement endeavor. Then there are those that relish the challenge and will meet and exceed his/her personal goals and become a police officer. May God watch over them.

A black police officer attempting to recruit minorities was asked by a St. Louis television reporter, "Is it cool to be a police officer today?" The officer replied, "It's not cool to be a cop today." Bullshit—it's always cool to be a cop!

The report continues to offer suggestions and ideas and make demands of the Ferguson police department. It uses the term "disparate impact" frequently. The writer of this tome apparently did not have access to a Thesaurus.

The DOJ final conclusion states:

Our investigation indicates that Ferguson as a city has the capacity to reform its approach to law enforcement. A small municipality department may offer greater potential for officers to form partnerships and have frequent, positive interactions with Ferguson residents, repairing and maintaining police-community relationships.

These reform efforts will be well worth the considerable time and dedication they will require, as they have the potential to make Ferguson safer and more united.

It appears that the Ferguson police department has a number of challenges it must address. This falls to the command structure of the police department and city management, challenges that are difficult but attainable. All the issues identified in the report must be addressed and some implemented, all with the goal of delivering first class law enforcement to ALL Ferguson citizens.

SOME TRUTHS ABOUT FERGUSON

The media continues its assault on police officers as a result of the Ferguson incident, as well as Staten Island, New York, and Baltimore. Officers and like-minded civilians feel the frustration and anger, because of the manner in which the profession is being portrayed. Random thoughts about the situation.

There will be more. Baltimore is only the last of a number of these type of incidents that will occur within the next (insert your own timetable here). We all know it's going to happen. Why you may ask? Good question. With somewhere in the vicinity of one million police officers in the United States and God only knows how many violent criminals in this nation, it won't take long until there is another confrontation. The result could mirror those of the instances in Ferguson or anywhere USA.

For the sake of argument, let's say a white cop kills another black criminal/thug. Once again, the media will portray the bad guy as a "gentle giant/midget/average size chump." The media will listen to the most outrageous and scandalous tales. They will take these tall tales and report them as fact. Even when the facts are found to be in direct contrast to the initial false reports, do not expect an apology or retraction of any previous broadcasts.

Eventually the truth will come out, as is the case in Ferguson where our president and attorney general knew early on that the use of force by then Ferguson police officer, Darren Wilson, was justified. The leaders of our country and assorted politicians used the report on the Ferguson police department to overshadow the report on the justified use of force. Both reports came out the same day, but listeners seldom heard that Wilson used force in a judicious manner.

Just think of the civil strife and conflict that could have been avoided, if anybody from the Department of Justice or the White House would have come out early in the investigation and told the nation the truth. Calming and healing words from either the president or the attorney general would have certainly had a soothing effect on the country.

This never changes. Truth comes out and police officers across the country have to deal with the consequences, good or bad. It seems like the bad stuff outweighs the good—something we all have to get used to. Maybe so, but perhaps a bit of unbiased reporting would refresh the population and lend a degree of creditability to the media.

The public will listen to those who speak to them. The media knows that a department spokesperson or commander cannot divulge any information about an investigation. This certainly does not stop reporters from sticking a mic in the face of a detective or a member of the command staff demanding an answer. Why? Because it looks good to the viewing public. At least, that's what the marketing people tell everybody. The attention span of any red-blooded American is that of a mosquito. The most recent incident and the truths behind it are soon forgotten, so the media continues to feed the information machine.

Having something to report seems way more important than waiting for the facts.

Politicians and activists always play to the crowd—many times, just to get their mug in front of a TV camera. Race baiter/race haters are like bad weather, they are always around. Anytime an incident occurs, we can all guess who's going to show up. Hugging the family and friends making a number of unwanted and unnecessary appearances. Oh yeah, a passionate plea, asking for legal tender. Weak-kneed companies and individuals usually give in. Probably with the question … how much to make this pest go away. Note to targets of this elaborate scam-o-rama … it's never enough.

As a general rule, the public does not understand use of force. Heaven forbid the use of deadly force. It's the department's job to educate the public. The latest incidents could have been avoided if the subject of the police action would have just complied. It's not rocket science everybody. Just comply and avoid an unpleasant situation. Police officers will not ask a person to do anything unreasonable. Police are not the jack-booted, foul-mouthed racists that the media would have you believe. Who'd a thunk it … "Hey guys, how about using the sidewalk?" Something this simple would lead to the upheaval and rioting in Ferguson and throughout the nation. But then, unemployed goofs have nothing better to do with their time.

Police officers cannot control what happens—they can only choose how they react to a situation. The Baltimore police officers were told to stand down during the beginning of the civil unrest. Teenagers and others threw rocks and anything they could get their grubby hands on at retreating police officers. The collective thought process of the police officers was, "Let's get these jerks and lock 'em up."

But no, the mayor of Baltimore told the cops to lay off. She also said at a news conference later that she " ... wanted to give those that wanted to destroy room to do that." What?

One can certainly understand why CVS drug stores would choose not to rebuild its burned and looted store that served a population in need of such services.

What faces police officers in the future? Use of force incidents will continue. Stay strong and resolute. Cops cannot be afraid to do their job. Act as the professionals you are. Criminals love lazy cops. Our nation's police officers cannot fall into the trap of only doing the minimum necessary. Everybody must remember why they went through all the BS to get the job. All the BS that goes with the job and the stress on family and friends. Why are there somewhere in the vicinity of one hundred applications for every one position that's open? Because even in today's environment, some people just want to be police officers. The background investigation, lie detector and psychological exams will weed out many—hopefully, those that feel a badge and gun are entitlements. They're not. They are symbols of a proud profession with a storied past and the ability to weather this storm. A calling that is honorable, valuable and necessary, especially to those in the worst sections of any major city. One can only hope this period of anti-police thinking passes quickly and police officers throughout the nation can continue to "SERVE AND PROTECT."

WHO SAYS I'M SORRY?

Immediately after the Michael Brown shooting and the false representation of the "Hands Up, Don't Shoot" took hold and spread throughout the country, our president and the US attorney general took to the airwaves. Not to ask for calm in the face of mounting demonstrations that had the potential and eventually did become violent, causing untold damage to property, in addition to the murder of two police officers in New York City and the shooting of two officers at the scene of the Ferguson demonstrations.

While the FBI and St. Louis county police investigations, underway in the Ferguson shooting of Michael Brown, Jr, both law enforcement organizations quickly determined that the shooting, condemned by many, was found to be justified, vindicating Ferguson police officer, Darren Wilson, under Missouri as well as federal law.

Our then attorney general, Eric Holder, met with the family of Michael Brown, Jr. One can understand the compassion for a lost loved one. After the meeting, he took a few questions at an impromptu news conference. He said, "I have assigned the justice department's most experienced investigators and prosecutors to the investigation." In addition, Mr. Holder promised a "fair and thorough" investigation.

The statements were made twelve days after the shooting incident. The investigating agencies preliminary conclusion was that what really occurred was that Michael Brown attacked the officer and attempted to take his gun. The only reason for that would be to kill the officer.

By his actions, Michael Brown, Jr. died as a result of his behavior against Officer Darren Wilson. Police react to an individual's actions. Michael Brown, Jr. didn't have to die on that hot August day in Ferguson, Missouri.

Mr. Holder continued in his self-serving statement, "We have seen great progress over the years. But we also see problems and these stem from mistrust and mutual suspicion."

Holder spoke of profiling. No mention of profiling made until the attorney general alluded to it. Often during the hours of darkness, police officers do not know the race of the people in the vehicle they are stopping.

Holder recounted stories of racially profiling himself.

"I think about my time in Georgetown—a nice neighborhood of Washington—and I am running to a motion picture at about eight o'clock at night. I am with my cousin. Police car comes driving up, flashes his lights, yells 'Where you going? Hold it.' I say, 'Whoa, I'm going to a movie.' Now my cousin started mouthing off, but I'm like, 'This is not where we want to go. Keep quiet.' I'm angry and upset. We negotiate the whole thing and we walk to our movie. At the time that he stopped me, I wasn't a kid. I wasn't a kid—I was a federal prosecutor. I worked at the United States Department of Justice. So I've confronted this behavior myself."

While Mr. Holder is bemoaning his contact with members of law enforcement, he stated he is an assistant US attorney. As such, Mr. Holder had contact with police officers and other enforcement personnel on a regular basis. Our then attorney general may have had contact with command staff of the DC police department. If not, he certainly had the ability to contact upper management and detail what occurred. There is no mention of any action taken to resolve the matter. An assistant US attorney is a powerful position. When managers of an organization are contacted, they sit up and take notice. A request for clarification of this matter to the justice department remains unanswered.

"The tensions between law enforcement and residents that erupted after the killing of Michael Brown, an unarmed, black teenager in Missouri, were unsurprising given the 'toxic' environment created by the biases of the Ferguson police department," he said.

This after the justice department issued a report that the department would not be filing any charges against former officer Darren Wilson.

Mr. Holder dwelled on the report on the Ferguson police department, rather than the report that the officer used deadly force in a lawful manner.

Our former attorney general used the March 4, 2014 report on the Ferguson police department to show "anecdotal" evidence of all manner of racial bias of the FPD—the operative term being anecdotal.

Additionally he stated, "We are prepared to use all the power that we have … to ensure that the situation changes there. We would use its full authority to demand police reforms in Ferguson, Missouri, including going so far as dismantling the department accused of racial bias."

Did Mr. Holder overlook the report on the shooting by Ferguson police officer Darren Wilson and focus almost entirely, on the FPD report? The report that showed Darren Wilson acted properly. That the "Hands Up, Don't Shoot," slogan is totally bogus.

How early in the investigation did he know about the legitimate use of force by Officer Wilson? Holder stated at the initiation of the FBI/Civil Rights Division investigation that he is briefed daily.

Upon knowing that the "Hands Up, Don't Shoot" mantra is based on false and misleading testimony, why didn't he or our president advise the nation? As a country, we all have the right to know. As the former attorney general, he has the duty and responsibility to tell the nation. Had he taken the high road and divulged information gained during the lawful investigation, this may have calmed a land in turmoil. A country wanting, desiring, and having a deep need for healing statements that did not come. Our former attorney general failed in not providing pertinent, factual information and data that clearly spelled out the events that took place on that hot, sticky day in August on the streets of Ferguson.

Comes Now Our President

On September 28, 2014, President Obama said, "The shooting death of a black teen by a white police officer last month in Ferguson, Missouri, exposed the racial divide in the American justice system that stains the hearts of black children." Here's a bulletin, Mr. President, it stains the hearts of all children.

"In too many communities around the country, a gulf of mistrust exists between local residents and law enforcement. Too many young men of color feel targeted by law enforcement—guilty of walking while black or driving while black, judged by stereotypes that fuel fear and resentment and hopelessness."

In the audience, Michael Brown's parents listened while our president intoned, "We have to close the gap—how justice is applied, but also how it's perceived, it's experienced. That's what we saw in Ferguson this summer when Michael Brown was killed and a community was divided. There are significant racial disparities in the criminal justice system in everything from enforcing drug policy to applying the death penalty to pulling people over."

"That has a corrosive effect," the president said. "The worst part of it is children grow unnecessarily fearful of somebody who doesn't look like them. Black children who feel as if no matter what he does, he'll be under suspicion. This is not the society we want, it is not the society our children deserve."

True, Mr. President, it is not the society we want. When he spoke shortly after the shooting incident, he could have said encouraging words. Something like … "I'm black and I'm the president of all the people … "

"Only in this country can a person from moderate means grow up to become the president … the land of opportunity, all you have to do is apply yourself." Something, anything, but the racially dividing narrative he and his minions put out to the nation.

"Michael Brown did not have his hands up and did not say, 'Don't shoot.' He attempted to gain control of the officer's weapon … " The truth.

Our president spoke too soon. Without knowing the facts, both Messrs. Obama and Holder gave false and misleading information to our anguished country. They are, after all, the president and former attorney general for all the people.

Not to be left out of the equation, Missouri governor, Jay, Ah … Um, Nixon, sided with the rioters and spoke of the "besmirching of Michael Brown's character" on the Sunday talk shows after the incident. Old Ah … Um prayed with Brown's family. This is compassionate and understandable.

Did he ever pray with Darren Wilson after determining that he acted within the law? Did he ever write a letter or note to the former officer saying he prayed for him? Probably not. The governor took the low road. He trashed the police, not just Ferguson, all cops associated with the Ferguson situation. He said he did not have faith in the St. Louis county police investigation. Maybe he spoke way too soon. The investigation by the FBI and the STLCOPD were and are basically the same. The governor is an attorney. One would think that an attorney should have all the facts before pontificating on a situation—epecially a situation as volatile and incendiary as the Ferguson shooting of Michael Brown, Jr.

Did our president and former attorney general write or speak with